BRIELLE

NEW JERSEY

UNION LANDING HISTORICAL SOCIETY

BRIELLE

NEW JERSEY

SALTWORKS TO SUBURB

Charleston   London

THE
History
PRESS

Published by The History Press
Charleston, SC 29403
www.historypress.net

Copyright © 2009 by the Union Landing Historical Society
www.briellehistory.org

First published 2009

Manufactured in the United States

ISBN 978.1.59629.640.4

Library of Congress Cataloging-in-Publication Data

Shea, Ray.
Brielle : saltworks to suburb / Union Landing Historical Society.
p. cm.
Includes bibliographical references.
ISBN 978-1-59629-640-4
1. Brielle (N.J.)--History. 2. Brielle (N.J.)--Social life and customs. I. Title.
F144.B72S54 2009
974.9'46--dc22
2009012222

CONTENTS

ACKNOWLEDGEMENTS

Founded in 1973, the Union Landing Historical Society strives to preserve, protect and document the history of the borough of Brielle and the Brielle area. To that end, the society has thus far published two history books. The first was *A History of Brielle: Union Landing Revisited* (Valente Publishing, 1989), and the second was *Images of America—Brielle* (Arcadia Publishing, 2006). This edition of *Brielle: Saltworks to Suburb* is the continuation of those previous efforts.

No project of this magnitude would have been possible without the cooperation of many individuals in many ways. I am most grateful to my wife, Suzanne, and our two children, Indigo and Miles, for their patience, love and support throughout this project. I am also deeply indebted to my fellow committee members for their hard work and dedication to our project: Betty Anderson, John Belding, E. David DuPre, Natalie and Richard Holmquist, Oliver Reynolds and Janice Wurfel.

The foundation of this work was laid in the society's first publication, *Union Landing Revisited*. We continue the work of those society members who embarked on the mission to preserve and record the history of Brielle. I would also like to acknowledge the contributions of many other individuals and groups: Barbara Reynolds and the Squan Village Historical Society, Sherri Hopkins, Borough Administrator Tom Nolan, Chief Michael Palmer and the Brielle Police Department, the Brielle Public Works Department, the Brielle Fire Company, the Brielle Chamber of Commerce, Marguerite "Peg" Beckett, Bob Sauer, Ethel D'Aloia Giaimo, Gail Herbert, Jackie Morgan, Beverly Mack, Diane and Glenn Miller, Edith Nowels, Joe Tonkovich and my ever vigilant proofreaders Judie and Joe Entwistle. Without their generosity in lending and donating photographs and archival materials, sharing their experiences and recognizing the importance of preserving the past for future generations this book would not have been possible.

ACKNOWLEDGEMENTS

Lastly, we are all indebted to the legacy of the late Helen Dennett Holmquist, who in 1962 compiled and published the first written history of Brielle.

Raymond F. Shea
President, Union Landing Historical Society

STATISTICS AND FACTS ABOUT BRIELLE

The borough of Brielle occupies 2.4 square miles in the southeast corner of Monmouth County, New Jersey. One can locate Brielle on a map at latitude 40°6′30″ north and longitude 74°3′44″ west. Brielle is bounded by Wall Township to the north and west, Manasquan Borough to the north and east and Point Pleasant and Point Pleasant Beach across the Manasquan River to the south. Within the boundaries of Brielle are approximately 4 miles of coastline. This entire coastline is considered riverfront, bordering the Manasquan River and its related estuaries—the Glimmer Glass, Crabtown Creek and Debbie's Creek. Brielle does not abut the Atlantic Ocean at any point, but it is within 1 mile of the open ocean via the Manasquan Inlet. Many locations along Brielle's coast offer access to the ocean without any drawbridge restrictions. Brielle's maritime placement is unique in another respect. With the completion of the Point Pleasant Canal in 1926, Brielle was connected by waterway to the northern portion of Barnegat Bay in Ocean County. Over the succeeding years, the Army Corps of Engineers gradually completed a protected inland waterway known as the Intracoastal Waterway. This passage formed a protected route that enabled mariners to voyage south to Florida and north to the Manasquan Inlet with a minimum of exposure to the open ocean. The importance of this could not be underestimated in the dangerous times of World War II.

The geographical boundaries of Brielle also include an uninhabited island situated in the Manasquan River about a mile and a half from the inlet mouth. Identified on most maps as Neinstedt Island or sometimes Osborn Island, it is almost universally known by its popular nickname, Treasure Island. Originally part of the vast landholdings of the local Osborn family, title to the island changed hands several times. At one point in time, a developer proposed purchasing the island and building homes on it after connecting it to the mainland with a private causeway. The last private owners of the land, the Neinstedt family, finally settled the question of development by deeding the property to the Borough of Brielle with the provision that if any development occurred on the island, title would revert to the Neinstedt heirs.

The mean elevation of Brielle is reported to be sixteen feet above sea level, but this average number comes about from two wide extremes. Being a coastal town, Brielle's lowest elevation is that of sea level. The highest point in Brielle, however, holds a unique geographical distinction. Located on the west side of Oceanview Road near a property line, there is a marker placed by the U.S. Geological Survey identifying the spot, at an elevation of ninety-five feet above sea level, as the highest point on the U.S. eastern seaboard between Brielle, New Jersey, and Key West, Florida. There are few points farther north, such as the Twin Lights in Atlantic Highlands, that are at a higher elevation than the Brielle marker, but all elevations south of Brielle within proximity to the coast are lower. The next highest coastal point south is on the island of Cuba.

As of 2007, Brielle's population was reported at 4,879.

CHAPTER 1

THE LENNI-LENAPE AND EUROPEAN COLONIZATION

THE PREHISTORY OF UNION LANDING

The Lenape Indians

Before the first Europeans came to New Jersey, there were many Indians living a peaceful and contented life here. Their needs were few and nature supplied all their wants. The woods gave them animals, nuts, berries and roots, and the waters gave them fish. The land, which they cultivated with their stone and wood tools, provided them with corn, beans, squash, pumpkins and other food.

The Lenape Indians of New Jersey, numbering between eight and ten thousand just prior to the arrival of the first white settlers, lived in small camps along the rivers and streams of New Jersey, eastern Pennsylvania and New York.

Coming up the Manasquan River, the first Europeans would have seen the one-room bark huts haphazardly strung along the banks of the river. The greatest surprise must have been the complete absence of metal weapons and domestic utensils commonly used in Europe. Native artifacts were fashioned from stone, bone, wood, shell and clay. The principal weapon was a bow made of pliable wood and fitted with a bowstring of twisted deerskin. The arrows were tipped with sharp points of flint. There were no wheeled vehicles, no horses, no cotton, wool or silk; no glass, gold or silver; and no precious stones.

To the Europeans, the Indian way of life must have seemed strangely primitive, but at the same time they realized that in their size and anatomy the Indians differed little from themselves. The average height of the males ranged from about five feet, seven inches to five feet, ten inches, although there were as many exceptions among the natives as there were among the Europeans. It did not take long to recognize, however, that the Indians were strong, quick on their feet, capable of long endurance and certainly better adapted than Europeans to survive in a woodland environment. Their features were coarse, with straight black hair, tan to red skin, prominent cheekbones and small dark eyes. The contrasting whiteness of their teeth was enhanced by their natural diet, although cavities were frequent, as archaeological evidence indicates.

Indians with beards were rare because hair grew sparsely on their faces, and it was their custom to use a hinged mussel shell like tweezers to pull any hair out by the roots. By removing the hair, they had smoother faces to paint when they decorated themselves for festivals and ceremonial dances. Painting the face with white, red and yellow clay, wooden ashes, black shale or the juices of herbs and berries was a custom practiced by both men and women. The colors had a special meaning. White, for example, was a symbol of happiness and peace. Black represented grief, evil and death. Red seems to have been a favorite color for the women. They reddened their eyelids, dabbed circular red spots on their cheeks and sometimes outlined the rims of their ears in red. Both men and women practiced tattooing, usually a snake, bird or animal representation, an act that was accomplished by puncturing the skin with flint or sharp stone and then rubbing powdered tree bark or paint into the abrasions.

Native clothing was made of animal skins, feathers and plant fibers. The women sewed the skins together with thread made of sinew, hair or tough grass. They punched holes in the hide with a deer bone and cut the skins with a stone knife. In the summer, the Indian male wore either an apron or loincloth made of soft deerskin that passed between his legs and was brought up and folded to hang from his deerskin belt, front and back. In the winter he wore a robe, usually of bearskin, thrown over one shoulder, leaving free the other arm, on which he sometimes wore a sleeve of animal skin. Leggings of buckskin kept his legs warm during the cold weather, and his moccasins made of deerskin were often decorated with shell beads or porcupine quills. The women wore knee-length skirts of deerskin, and their breasts were bare. Long, braided hair set off their soft features. They used bear grease as a hair dressing, and men as well as women applied it to their bodies as an insect repellant. The women wore bands of wampum beads around their foreheads, and both men and women adorned themselves with gorgets, pendants, beads, necklaces, armbands, anklets and earrings of stone, shells, animal teeth and claws. In the winter, the women covered their breasts and shoulders with shawls of animal pelts and robes of turkey feathers. The feather robes were so neatly and expertly made that the feathers formed a smooth, downy surface to shed rain and protect the wearer from the cold. In

The Lenni-Lenape and European Colonization

Lenape Indians harvested and smoked shellfish along the banks of the Manasquan River for generations prior to the arrival of Europeans in the region.

cold weather the women also protected their legs with deerskin leggings and their feet with moccasins.

The Indians' source of food came from gathering, fishing, agriculture and hunting. Some sources of food were natural and could usually be found in the area in which they lived. Here they could find persimmons, grapes, plums, beans, nuts, seeds and perhaps strawberries, blackberries, raspberries, huckleberries and, in some areas, cranberries. Depending on the season, men and boys would go fishing and hunting, tasks that would often take them away from their homes for extended periods of time. While fishing could often be done in nearby streams or rivers, surf fishing could require some travel. Hunting would be done in more remote areas that were reserved by common agreement among neighboring Indians. Some hunting, depending on the season, was done in family territories and dogs were used. While the dog was domesticated, he was never regarded as a pet. Deer, elk and bear became the quarry. Smaller game, such as squirrels, rabbits and the like, as well as wild turkeys, were also taken. Boys were trained for hunting and were proficient by age fifteen. After the hunt, the meat was cut and dried in the sun until cured.

Agriculture gradually outranked hunting as the primary source of food, but the planting and harvesting of crops became mostly women's work. The principal crops were maize, beans, pumpkins and tobacco. Men cleared the land of trees and brush, burning them and mixing the ashes into the soil.

Homes were usually built on bluffs beyond flood areas but near to the woods that would provide convenient sources of firewood and game. Some shelters were rectangular with arched roofs, measuring about ten feet in height. Other shelters were circular with arched roofs, measuring about ten by twenty feet. The insides were simple, containing raised wooden benches that were used as tables, seats and beds. There were two meals a day, taken while sitting on the ground and served from clay cooking pots with wooden ladles.

Burial customs among the Indians may have changed from generation to generation and were probably influenced by other Indians. In some instances, graves were dug within the occupied area of a village; in others, there was a burial ground beyond the bounds of the village. Bodies were placed in graves in both flexed and sometimes extended positions. At some sites, disarticulated bones of the deceased were buried in nests or bundles, and the remains of a number of individuals were placed in the same grave. Pipes, shell beads, pottery and stone artifacts are often found in some graves, but in others, no artifacts are present.

Archaeological Studies

Sometime during the middle of the twentieth century, as the western part of Brielle was being developed, in the woods adjacent to an old Indian lake site near the bend on Riverview Drive, an unusual find was unearthed. What appeared to be arrowheads were discovered. To confirm the authenticity of the find, persons in the community who were thought to be more knowledgeable about such things were asked to evaluate the find. In the opinion of these "experts," the articles were declared "genuine."

As word of the discovery gradually spread, curiosity seekers with shovels began to appear. Most were amateurs, but in time more serious and knowledgeable devotees came upon the scene. It wasn't, however, until the spring of 1975 that the Brielle Environmental Commission, under the chairmanship of Richard Scott, became concerned about the possible loss of this cultural resource. With financial backing from the Women's Club of Brielle, the Brielle Environmental Commission contracted the Archaeological Research Center at Seton Hall University to do an archaeological appraisal of the site.

Excavation began on Saturday, May 10, 1975, with archaeologist Herbert C. Kraft heading up the six-member team. Several ten- by ten-foot test squares were laid out and examined, but as the report states:

The Lenni-Lenape and European Colonization

The archaeological locus that is herein named the Brielle site could have been one of the more significant prehistoric aboriginal culture areas of the east coast of New Jersey. Instead, it has become a testimonial to the thoughtless and irresponsible destruction of an irreplaceable cultural/historical resource. Like so many prehistoric sites, it has been known and surface collected for nearly a century by irresponsible amateurs.

Nevertheless, continued professional excavations eventually were able to provide some insights with respect to the presumed stratigraphy and deposition of the artifacts. At these locations, prehistoric artifacts were encountered in the upper enriched zones being excavated. From these artifacts, and the collections of other reputable collectors, an attempt was made to reconstruct the prehistoric activities of the Brielle site.

The Brielle site on today's Birch Drive was a camp used for many thousands of years by the Indians during their hunting and fishing trips, possibly as many as eight thousand years ago. The debris and surviving artifacts that were found best represent the time of the late Woodland period (circa AD 1000–1700).

Most of the historic artifacts were found in the top, or humus-enriched, zone of excavations. Numerous shells and shell fragments were found scattered throughout the soil. Chips of stone, arrowheads, scrapers, knives, hammers, axes and pottery shards were all that remained of the Indians in the way of their tools. Local collectors discovered a single burial many years ago. It was the grave of an Indian woman who died sometime after 1695. This is known because a pipe made in Scotland after that date was found with her in the grave.

The stone chips tell the archaeologist that the Indians made tools and sharpened them. The arrowheads were used for hunting deer and other animals that once lived in the area. Scrapers and knives were used in cutting meat and for cleaning animal skins for the making of clothing. Hammers, stones and axes were used perhaps to clear the land of trees, to build houses and to make canoes for river travel.

From the many shells found, the archaeologist can tell that the Indians did considerable shellfishing while they lived in the area of present-day Brielle. The many fragments of pottery and the fire-cracked stones also tell of the cooking, and perhaps the drying and smoking, of shellfish for later use.

The excavations also suggest that the most extensive settlement was from about six hundred to eight hundred years ago. The presence of stemmed and notched projectile points indicates that the Indians had been hunting and camping in the area of Brielle for many thousands of years. The evidence

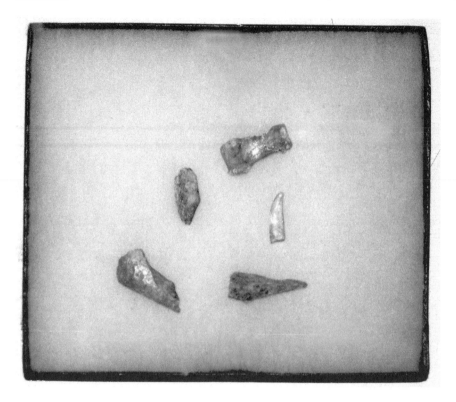

Bone and tooth fragments found at the Brielle site.

suggests, however, that the settlement's use was seasonal. The Lenape came to this site in the spring and early summer and returned to northern inland settlements in the late summer and fall.

In 2005, the Cultural Resources Consulting Group of Highland Park, New Jersey, completed a second archaeological dig, commissioned by William Rathjen, who is a major developer of property in the western end of Brielle. The project, headed by archaeologist Charles Bello and his team, further explored the Birch Drive site. They unearthed many artifacts similar to the ones produced in the first dig by archaeologist Herbert C. Kraft of Seton Hall University. A selection of these artifacts is on public display in the borough hall, adjacent to the office of Brielle Borough Historian John Belding.

These flint arrow points are representative of the types of stone tools unearthed at the Birch Drive camp.

In 2005, an organized archaeological dig was conducted at the Birch Drive site by Charles Bello. Many artifacts similar to the previous dig were discovered, but nothing truly unique was found. The site is now cleared for development.

EUROPEAN COLONIZATION

In Europe, as the fifteenth century approached, the established patterns of trade routes to the Orient were beginning to be challenged. Bandits were attacking caravans. Cargo was being stolen in huge quantities and drivers were being slain. Thinking was now being directed toward finding new routes to the East.

Spain and Portugal, spurred on by the high costs of obtaining spices, silks and other products of the Orient, set about seeking their own trade routes. Portuguese explorer Vasco de Gama sailed around the southern tip of Africa, across the Indian Ocean and reached the western coast of India. Spain, however, pursued a risky and controversial plan to sail directly westward across the Atlantic to reach the Orient. With Columbus's discovery of a new land, both countries' whole focus now centered on what was to be the fruit of this amazing discovery. Consequently, by the Treaty of Todesillas (1494), these two Iberian nations warned that they planned to monopolize the fruits of their discoveries in Central America and the Caribbean, to the exclusion of the rest of the world. Nevertheless, England and Holland, having become commercial powers, proceeded to establish settlements farther north on the continent. With the defeat of the Spanish Armada in 1588, colonization of the New World by other nations became inevitable. As the seventeenth century dawned, settlers from other European nations, including the Swedes, French, Dutch, Welsh, Germans and Scotch, came with their own diversified backgrounds to settle in this New World.

While colonization throughout the New World would proceed on a wide scale, we will be focusing our attention on the beginning of settlements along a section of the East Coast of North America that at a later time would come to be called New Jersey. These settlements lie between the Hudson and Delaware Rivers, known to the Dutch as North River and South River.

As the United Netherlands, the Dutch were becoming a wealthy and culturally advanced nation. They already carried on extensive commerce and had hired an Englishman, Henry Hudson, to expand their horizons. Hudson's employment was with the Dutch East India Company. He would command the *Half Moon*, sailing the waters of the northern seas. Turning south, he came upon the mouth of the Delaware River and dropped anchor, planning to go ashore. The curious natives at first welcomed his party. Later, after exploring a large river that would in time come to be called Hudson's River, and experiencing some difficulties with the Indians, Hudson sailed for home. It wasn't until 1614 that another company, the United Netherlands

Company, was organized and, upon returning to America, established a trading settlement.

In 1626, Peter Minuet purchased land on Manhattan Island from the Indians, and in 1629 his company instituted a patroon system, giving land to anyone who would bring colonists to settle there. The settlers in most of the colonies along the eastern coast of North America were overwhelmingly English. In order to develop colonies and to eliminate Dutch competition, their Stuart kings divided their lands among powerful trading companies and individual proprietors, to whom they gave certain governmental powers with the authority to administer and advance their objectives. Boards of privy councilors were also appointed and even given the power to remove colonial governors as they saw fit. But because colonial government was working out rather well, the councilors developed a tendency not to interfere.

In 1664, the Duke of York divided his domain in the New World between his close friends Lord John Berkeley and Sir George Carteret and gave them certain governmental powers. Carteret, a native of the Isle of Jersey, had protected Charles II while he was staying on the isle. As a reward, Carteret was given an isle off the coast of Virginia to be named New Jersey. Carteret sent out an expedition to colonize this island, but his ship was captured by the Cromwellians and the effort was abandoned. It is doubtless that with some remembrance of this previous grant the new colony on the mainland came to be called New Jersey.

In April 1665, a group of settlers received from Colonel Richard Nicolls vast tracts of land that eventually became the townships of Shrewsbury and Middletown. Nicolls had received from the Duke of York wide latitude in administrating the duke's property in the New World. A section of Shrewsbury would eventually be split off in 1801 to become Howell Township. In 1851, the eastern portion of Howell would be separated to form Wall Township. The borough of Brielle would later secede from Wall in 1919.

In the meantime, Berkeley and Carteret drew up a constitution, known as the Concessions and Agreement of 1665, in which liberal political and religious privileges were offered to attract prospective immigrants to settle in the colony. The settlers were not permitted to purchase their lands but were required to pay an annual quitrent. This provision caused major dissent among those who received land grants from Colonel Nicolls and those who purchased their lands directly from the Indians. It was the contention of the latter that the land grant system, as provided in the Concessions and Agreement document, did not apply to them.

An attempt was made to resolve this problem on March 25, 1670, since this date was the day quitrents were due. Townspeople who refused to take out proprietary patents for their lands alleged that the titles for the lands they received by way of grants from Nicolls or by deeds from the Indians were all that they needed. Accordingly, they refused to pay any quitrents, and furthermore, ever since their arrival in New Jersey they believed that they were entitled to manage their own affairs.

Unexpectedly, on July 30, 1673, a Dutch squadron from the West Indies surprised an English garrison at New York and compelled its surrender, at which point New Jersey was once more under the Dutch flag. When peace was eventually restored, Philip Carteret once again took over as governor and New Jersey was again under proprietary control. With Sir George Carteret in charge of the East Jersey province, it was now decreed that only those who held proprietary patents would have the full rights of freeholders. The people acquiesced and paid the hated quitrents. Still today, in East Jersey all land titles derive from proprietary patents and any title to unclaimed or disputed land can only be obtained through the Board of Proprietors in Perth Amboy, the original capital of East Jersey.

Over the ensuing years, with increased migration of people from New York and New England, Shrewsbury became a sizable township, with farms ranging from one hundred to two hundred acres in size.

Shortly afterward, there emerged two different types of landholding—small homesteads in towns and vast tracts of lands held by the proprietors in rural areas. At the same time, population shifted from those who migrated from other colonies to an influx of English and Scottish settlers with differing religious denominations. This resulted in a fairly diverse population.

With the influx of English settlers, a new level of government was instituted in 1683. This was the county level, coming between township and provincial authority exactly as it did in England. Later, when proprietors were forced to surrender their governmental authority, New Jersey became a royal colony.

Royal control centered on constitutional authority, and while accepted for a time as providing greater stability, royal control came to be regarded as too complex and restrictive. The royal governor, while enjoying personal authority, exercised his authority through appointments of officials and the veto of proposed legislation. Nevertheless, he had to work through the assembly, which would jealously defend and attempt to expand its privileges. The assembly was a body to be reckoned with since it controlled the purse strings. On the other hand, the governor and his council were given the authority to hear appeals from decisions of the Supreme Court and could have the final say. New York and New Jersey shared the same governor until 1738, at which time New Jersey was given its own.

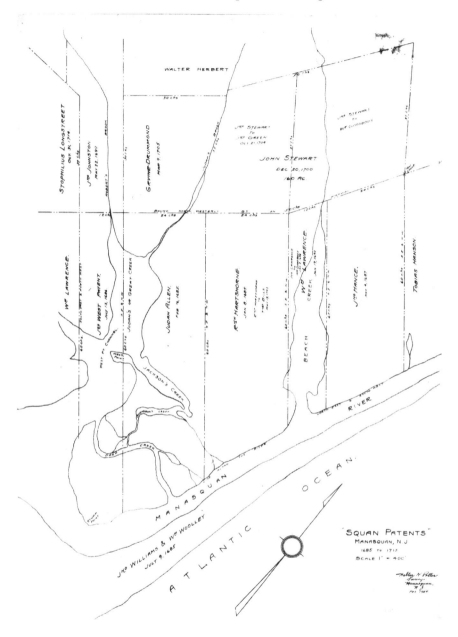

This early map of the Manasquan River coastline in Brielle shows how the land was divided into narrow rectangular parcels by the original Proprietors of East Jersey.

This early stone survey marker bears the initials A.O. on one side and J.O. on the other side. It marks the separation of property once owned by James and Abraham Osborn, the sons of Revolutionary War veteran Lieutenant Abraham Osborn. It sits on a property line that dates back to the original divisions by the Proprietors of East Jersey.

All of these complications made it increasingly clear that the original Concessions and Agreement of 1665 had been, in fact, the source of the rights and privileges that the settlers believed had been granted to them. The assembly was considered the voice of the people, and the people were now cultivating the ideas of self-government.

CHAPTER 2

COLONIAL LIFE IN UNION LANDING

Aprime consideration for any settler was an evaluation of a prospective site to determine what natural features it possessed. The first settlers in the Landing section of Shrewsbury Township found a tract of land adjacent to the Manasquan River, which emptied into the ocean. Waterpower from rivers is essential for the operation of sawmills and gristmills. If the river was fresh water, it might be a source for drinking water, cooking, bathing and, perhaps, cleaning or washing. But because tides and winds affect boating, there had to be an alternative for traveling and shipping.

Settlers made the best of roads such as they were, with ruts in the winter and quagmires in the spring and summer. Most of them were simply Indian trails through the woods. Local roads were few and poorly maintained. Highways were slightly better and were the prime location for taverns and inns, providing food, drink and lodging for wagon travelers. Wagons of the time had wooden wheels and crude benches and were usually left in open space near the stables. The taverns really became social centers where locals and travelers exchanged news or discussed politics. They also became sites for celebrations, dances and meetings.

Most settlers made their living by farming their own lands or working as tenant farmers on large estates. Since labor-saving machinery did not exist, the clearing of land required backbreaking efforts. Plows were drawn by horses. Most crops were harvested by hand scythes or by family teams who handpicked them. At the Landing, a few local sea captains engaged in the shipping of crops and other local products to nearby markets in New York and Philadelphia. Fishing became a livelihood for many seamen.

There were few skilled craftsmen, but for these few there was strong demand for their services, which often were exchanged for payment in produce.

Formal religion in the area was almost nonexistent. There were very few churches, and those that did exist were at best nonfunctional because of the lack of trained clergymen and theological academies to train new clergy. On the other hand, many individual families had strong religious convictions that were observed within the family community, as evidenced by the spiritual quotations on the tombstones in our historical cemeteries.

Education also lagged. Outside of established towns there existed only scattered one- or two-room schoolhouses. Parents joined together to hire a schoolmaster, who would be responsible for instruction in basic studies to a widely divergent assembly of youngsters of different ages, training and background, as well as discipline.

From the time of the arrival of the white man in this area, relations with the Indians were generally friendly. As the area became more settled, the Indians gradually yielded their lands and left.

By the beginning of the American Revolution, about one-twelfth of the population was Negro, most of whom were slaves. Slavery was practiced in Union Landing, although in his will, written one hundred years before the Emancipation Proclamation, Samuel Osborn directed that his slaves be granted their freedom.

Union Road, now called Union Lane, is one of the oldest roads in present-day Brielle. It terminated at the Manasquan River, as it does today. This point of termination was the main point of access to the river and became known as "the landing." The settlement itself, because it had no other name, became known as "Landing."

At the time of the Revolution, the Landing area later known as Brielle consisted mainly of woods and farmland. There was much activity, with vessels coming and going at the Union Landing wharf and the Union Salt Works. The wharf was located at the end of Union Road and adjacent to the Union Salt Works on the riverfront along what is now Green Avenue. At that time, the only bridge across the Manasquan River was located more than one mile upriver in Allenwood. It was built in 1768 and used throughout the Revolution.

Sometime during the events leading toward union and independence, the patriotic inhabitants of Landing selected the name Union for their community. Possibly around this time, Union Lane received its present name. The landing at the foot of Union Lane continued in great use. It was the focal point for shipping and importing products of all kinds. The name Landing persisted, but since there were many "Landings," in order to clarify its location, it is probable that this landing on the Manasquan River was popularly called Union Landing. The earliest settlers known to us in what we now call Brielle were the Longstreets, the Osborns and the Allens. There were of course others, but very little information about them is available.

THE LONGSTREETS

The earliest known white settler was Dirck Stoffelse Langstraat, who came from Holland to America in 1657 and settled in Long Island. He purchased land in Shrewsbury Township, New Jersey, of which present-day Brielle was a part at that time. His son, Theophilus Stoffel Dircksen Langstraat, made his home on a plantation on the shore of the Manasquan River. He and his wife, Moyka Laen, had four sons and six daughters. Stoffel Langstraat died on the plantation around 1741, and his oldest sons, Dirck and Gilbert (or Gisbert), inherited the large property. Dirck married Alice Osborn, and they had four sons and five daughters. Gilbert married Rachel Schenck. They had two sons and five daughters.

By the time of the Revolution, the name had been Anglicized and the spelling "Longstreet" became standard. The following were some of the Longstreet men active in the rebel cause during the Revolution: Aaron Longstreet, lieutenant in the Monmouth Regiment and later captain in the Middlesex Regiment; Gilbert Longstreet, captain of Wyckoff's Company, State Troop; and Aaron and John Longstreet, privates of Captain Waddell's Company, First Regiment.

Dirck or Derrick Longstreet, son of Dirck and Alice Osborn Longstreet, married Prudence Parker. He is mentioned later in connection with the raid on the Union Salt Works. The couple had five sons and three daughters. The Christian name of Dirck, Derrick or Richard has been carried through to each generation. Their son William G. married Deborah Kinney on July 4, 1804. They had ten children, seven sons and three daughters: Alice, Mary, Elizabeth, Kinney, Moses, Joseph, John H., Tabor O., Carhart S. and William T. The generations of local Longstreets in the eighteenth and nineteenth centuries averaged nine children. Between today's Longstreet Avenue and Harris Avenue is a creek officially known as Longstreet Creek. It is popularly also known as Debbie's Creek. A local legend has it that this creek was so named because Debbie Longstreet flung herself into it to commit suicide upon her twelfth, sixteenth or twenty-fourth pregnancy, depending on the storyteller. Records show that Deborah Longstreet did not drown herself in the creek; rather, she outlived her husband by many years and became guardian of her minor children. She petitioned the Orphans Court of the County of Monmouth on October 24, 1835, for permission to sell a portion of the family real estate, a necessary procedure for a woman in those days, for the maintenance and education of the wards Tabor O. and Carhart S. Longstreet. The petition stated that these *wards had no personal estate that they are personally seized in fee simple of certain real estate in the Township of Howell which was set off to them in severally by metes and bounds by Commissioners appointed by Orphans Court to divide the real estate of their father William G. Longstreet deceased. And they have no other real estate. And that the said rents issues and profits of the said real estate of which said wards are seized…are not sufficient for their maintenance and education.*

The court agreed to the requested sale. The property is identified as being in Howell because at that time Union Landing was still part of Howell Township.

Another local legend deserves to be mentioned at this time. It is the story of Indian Will and the Longstreets. Will was a local Indian who frequently visited Dirck Longstreet's house. On one occasion, he showed Longstreet some silver coins. He told Longstreet that he had found them at the beach and that there were yellow ones also. They went to the beach and examined an old chest covered with a tarpaulin, which had been buried in the sand. Will liked the white coins better, so he kept them and gave Longstreet the yellow ones. And thus Longstreet became a wealthy man. True or not, it is certainly documented that the Longstreets owned vast tracts of land in the area. Their many descendants were very important in their own right. The large Longstreet holdings were eventually divided into today's building lots. Until the mid-twentieth century, the Longstreet family burial ground was located near the present intersection of Rankin Road and Schoolhouse Road. To facilitate construction of homes here following World War II, the remains were disinterred. Richard Longstreet, his wife Lydia, his second

The Longstreet Burial Ground once stood on the hilltop on what is known today as Rankin Road. Revolutionary War veterans and members of the Longstreet family, the area's first white settlers, were buried here. When the area began to be developed in the late 1940s, the remains were exhumed and reinterred at nearby Atlantic View Cemetery in Manasquan.

wife Zilpha, Garret Longstreet's wife Lydia and Willuam VanMater were removed to Atlantic View Cemetery along with their gravestones. They show dates of death from 1810 to 1863.

THE OSBORNS

The Osborn family, one of the earliest in the area, emigrated from England. Some early records show the name spelled Osborne, but the branch of the family that settled here did not spell the name with the final *e*. The Osborns first settled on Long Island and migrated to this area in the early 1700s. Samuel Osborn was definitely living here in 1754. His farmhouse still exists. Now part of a restaurant called Harpoon Willy's, it is located on the riverfront near the present Route 70 bridge. During the Revolution, Osborn's wife is said to have barred the door of the house with musket in hand, forbidding the British soldiers to cross the threshold. They did not enter but did steal cattle, horses and poultry.

Samuel's son Abraham, who was born in 1752, inherited large tracts of land in this area. The Osborn family owned and farmed many acres along both sides of the Manasquan River, including all of the land on which the Manasquan River Golf Club is located. Abraham Osborn's wife, Elizabeth Pintard Allen, was the sister of Captain Sam Allen. Throughout the Revolution, the lives of Abraham Osborn and Captain Sam Allen were often linked. Abraham Osborn served in the Third Regiment, Monmouth County Militia, having entered the military in the summer of 1776. His field officers were General Forman, Colonel Hendrickson and Captain Longstreet, who was succeeded by Captain Buckalew. Osborn was promoted to first lieutenant after a year of service and kept this rank until the war's end. Around 1780, Abraham and Elizabeth built the brick house that is now part of the Manasquan River Golf Club. Their son Abraham, born in 1784, inherited the house. The senior Abraham Osborn died of old age in 1835 and is buried in the small graveyard that he had established on his farm. Upon his death, via a will, he divided his farm among his sons. The share of the farm received by his son James included the family burial ground, marked today "Osborn Family Burial Ground," on Holly Hill Drive. The white clapboard house that belonged to James still stands and is located at what is now 915 Riverview Drive. Lieutenant Osborn and his wife had four sons and four daughters. The Osborn family prospered and left many descendants in this area. His wife was buried beside him in the family plot in 1840.

THE ALLENS

Allen family ancestors, originally from England, settled in New England. Around 1740, David Allen moved to New Jersey, acquired a large tract of land on the north bank of the Manasquan River and proceeded to cultivate it. His original home, upriver from the Osborns', was also near the present Route 70 bridge. His brother Joseph's son was General Ethan Allen of Vermont. David Allen had two sons, Adam and Samuel. Adam settled in Virginia; Samuel, a Quaker, inherited his father's property. Samuel's oldest son, also named Samuel, was born in 1757. He was later known as Captain Sam. In 1776, he married Elizabeth Fleming. Her brothers, Steven and Jacob, served in the Revolution with distinction.

At the start of the war, Captain Sam Allen, only eighteen years old, was left in charge of the "home guard," which was a group of volunteers formed to protect the residents of the area. British troops and Loyalists foraged around the countryside, plundering and stealing anything of value. Tories preyed on their rebel neighbors. This was, in fact, a civil war as well as an international one. Your next-door neighbor could be your enemy. Homes were burned, and stories of rape and murder were told in connection with these raids.

The settlers also had to deal with the Pine Barren Robbers, murderous cutthroats supposedly loyal to the Crown but who were really interested in their own profit. They would hide in the pine forests and swamps along the upper Manasquan River. Young Captain Sam Allen and his band of volunteers put up a brave fight against these foes.

Captain Allen's life was constantly in danger, as were those of his family. Three times his house was burned to the ground. Once he was captured, tied to a tree and threatened with death unless he revealed where his money was hidden, which he refused to do. He was then taken to the house of his brother-in-law Abraham Osborn, who was home on furlough. The troops surrounded Osborn's house and demanded his money. His wife, Elizabeth, screamed out the hiding place to save his life. The British had intended to take both Allen and Osborn prisoner, but they were rescued by friendly neighbors.

Captain Allen and his men often sailed from the Manasquan Inlet to protect the coasting schooners that carried farm products and livestock to New York and other ports for the use of the Patriots. His maritime exploits are well known. In his 1832 declaration to obtain a pension, Abraham Osborn related that he and Captain Allen and his group captured a British brig off Shrewsbury Inlet near the war's end.

Late on a summer day in 1782, Lieutenant Osborn and Captain Allen were captured by British and Tory forces. While being marched to Sandy Hook and imprisonment, they hatched a plan to escape when darkness fell near Shark River. They refused to continue marching unless they were unbound. The enemy reluctantly agreed, and the march continued. At an agreed signal, both men jumped to opposite sides of the path and disappeared into a thick growth of laurel and other bushes. The prisoners managed to escape in spite of heavy firing by the enemy. They both survived the war and returned to their lands.

Captain Allen continued managing his estate after the war. His wife died in 1800 and was buried under a tree on the Allen plantation. Captain Allen died in 1831 and was placed beside her. The location of their graves is unknown. The couple left many descendants, some of whom are still living in this area.

THE UNION SALT WORKS

A major contribution of Union Landing to the War for Independence was common salt. It is hard to understand today the importance of salt in Revolutionary times. Considering that there was no way to preserve food except by salting, smoking or drying, one can begin to understand its importance. There were no refrigerators or canned goods back then. Salt was also used to make foods that were often not very fresh more palatable. It is a common misconception that table salt was also used for the making of gunpowder. The common household salt is sodium chloride. Salts used for explosives are saltpeter or niter (potassium nitrate) and soda niter or Chile saltpeter (sodium nitrate).

Before the war, most salt was brought to America on British ships after it was harvested by evaporation on British colonies in the Caribbean. When the war broke out, the British placed an embargo on imported salt and the colonists were forced to find other sources of salt. Thus, they turned to their own local seawater. The salt shortage became so serious that on May 28, 1776, Congress approved a bounty for salt that could be smuggled through the British blockade or produced locally. Saltworks of various sizes were built up and down the coast. One of the largest was the Union Salt Works at Union Landing on the Manasquan River. It occupied about five acres along what is now Green Avenue, extending northward from Union Lane, which at one time was called the "Old Salt Road."

There is some confusion about who owned and/or operated the Union Salt Works. A deed in the Hall of Records in Freehold states that John Kaign, Caleb Newbold and others purchased three parcels of land composed of about five acres at the location from Richard Longstreet and Thomas

Tilton. Some of the land was purchased in 1776 and some in 1778. An order from the Proprietors dated August 1778 to survey the woodland adjacent to the Union Salt Works located on the north side of the Manasquan River states, however, that the works was "now carried on" by Hendrick Smock, Theophilus Little, Garret Longstreet and John Covenhoven. Advertisements and newspaper accounts related to the works carry the names John Kaign, Nethaniel Lewis and Joseph Newbold.

Some writers have stated that General David Forman may have been connected to the building of the works, but there is no proof of this. Horner's *This Old Monmouth of Ours* states that General Forman sent a memorandum to George Washington applying for a contract to supply the army with salt from works he and some others had invested in at Barnegat. Weiss's *The Revolutionary Salt Works of the New Jersey Coast* also states that General Forman told Washington that he and his associates were constructing saltworks on Barnegat Bay.

Salt was obtained from seawater by various methods. One obvious method was to allow salt water to flow into troughs at high tide and then close the ends of the troughs, letting the sun and breezes dry away the water. The Union Salt Works and other larger works drew the water up by windmill-powered pumps into large cisterns. The water was then put into copper or iron kettles or pans and boiled away. The remaining salt was packed into small barrels or baskets and transported overland by wagon and to various ports by salt schooners.

Salt sold at about thirty cents a bushel before the war. During the war, salt from the shore works cost about thirteen to fifteen dollars a bushel. Salt's scarcity resulted in great speculation. It sold for thirty-five dollars a bushel at Morristown at one time. There was great demand for it from the colonists as well as the Continental army.

The importance of these saltworks was such that men employed there were exempt from military service, and often forces of militia of twenty-five to forty-five men protected the larger works.

Sunday, April 5, 1778, is a date that stands out in the history of Union Landing. Despite the militia protecting the works, a force of about two hundred British troops from New York and marines and Loyalists from Sandy Hook sailed from the Hook for Squan Inlet for the purpose of destroying the saltworks there. They arrived at the inlet in the morning, and as described in the April 13, 1778 issue of the *New York Gazette and Weekly Mercury*:

> *The troops landed and marched up to some very considerable Salt-works, erected there by the Rebels, which they entirely demolished. There could not be less than One Hundred different Houses, in which of each were from*

six to ten Coppers and Kettles, for the Purpose of boiling salt…Besides demolishing the above Works, they destroyed immense Quantities of Salt, Beef, salted and fried Hams, Sides of Bacon, Flour, Corn, and Hay. They brought off a sloop belonging to Boston, partly loaded with flour and at three o'clock in the Afternoon re-embarked.

The *New Jersey Gazette* reported that the enemy burned all of the Union Salt Works and then burned all of the buildings except Derrick Longstreet's. There is also a letter from Kildare, Monmouth County, that states that Derrick's house was spared. For many years, it has been believed that the Derrick Longstreet house that was spared was the one at 532 Union Lane, known as Boxwood Cottage. In 1990, the house was examined by Gail Hunton, preservation specialist of the Monmouth County Park System, who estimated that it was built around 1820. Obviously, that house could not have been in existence during the Revolution. Another report says that the troops burned all of the buildings except "those belonging to one of the Longstreets, who was a Tory."

Colonel Israel Shreve, of the Second New Jersey Regiment, wrote to General George Washington to inform him of the destruction and request additional troops for the area.

> *Mount Holley April 7th 1778*
> *Sir*
> *This moment I Received Intilligence that the Enemy has landed at Squan between 600 and 1000 men and distroyed all the Salt and works in that Neighbourhood.*
>
> *If your Excy. should think proper to send more troops to this quarter, with Artillery, I Beg for the Jersey Comp'y of Artillery, at present Commanded by Capt. Seth Bowen,*
>
> *The spirit of Burning prevails still Among those Misarable Villans at billingsport, Last night they Come to Woodbury in a skulking manner and Burnt two Whig houses, and ordered other famalys to move out in a few days or they would burn them in them.*
> *I am your Excys very Humble Servt.*
> *I Shreve Col.*
> *Comdt.*

Derrick Longstreet must have been a passive Tory, since he was allowed to retain his property after the war. In his well-known book *This Old Monmouth of Ours*, William Horner states:

They were loyalists in principle, but not in practice. Some such "passive"
Tories lived in peace and honor among their friends and neighbors all
through the war, and resumed their rightful places in the activities of the
community at the close of the struggle.

The Union Salt Works must have been rapidly rebuilt, for it was advertising for woodcutters in March 1779. The ineffectiveness of the British blockade due to the naval skirmishes with the French fleet caused the price of salt to decline. The increase in salt production also affected the price. Several saltworks were put up for sale, including the Union Salt Works, which was advertised for sale by Nathaniel Lewis, Joseph Newbold and John Kaighn in the March 24, 1779 issue of the *New Jersey Gazette*. It was described as follows:

The works consist of a boiling-house, about 90 feet long and 33 feet wide,
in which are five copper and four iron pans, the copper weighing upwards

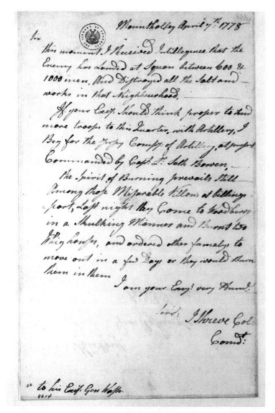

This is a photograph of the original letter from Colonel Israel Shreve to General George Washington detailing the first destruction of the Union Salt Works in 1778.

of 3,000 lb. four of which pans are round, about 6 feet diameter and about 12 inches deep, the other about 13 and a half feet long, 6 feet wide, and 14 inches deep. The iron pans are made of wrought iron plate near a quarter of an inch thick, two of them are about 12 feet long, 6 feet wide, and 14 inches deep; and the other two are each about 16 feet long, 6 feet wide, and 17 inches deep; all of which are fixed in the best manner for the business of salt-boiling. Adjoining to the boiling house is a convenient store-house, capable of containing 800 bushels of salt, and contiguous thereto is a pump-house in which are two pumps almost new, by which the water from the bay is conveyed either immediately into the pans, or into a covered cistern holding about 150 hogsheads, at times when the water is saltiest, and from thence let into the pans.

The lot of ground whereon these works stand contains about five acres of good land well-fenced, on which are also erected a dwelling-house, stables, smoke-house and other buildings, which are convenient. The dwelling house was lately erected, being about 35 by 24 feet, two stories high, with a cellar under the whole, and an excellent pump of fresh water at the door. The stables are likewise new, capable of holding about ten tons of hay, a considerable quantity of grain, and sufficient room for sixteen horses.

Will be disposed of with the above premises about 160 acres of land, wooded mostly with oak, about two miles and a half from the works.

At the same time and place will be sold about 20,000 good bricks, two horses, a cow and calf, a good wagon well ironed, a large well built scow, two bateaux in good repair, a quantity of old iron, and several small bars of blistered steel; also household goods and kitchen furniture, consisting of four feather beds with suitable bedding, bedsteads, with many other articles.

The works and buildings are pleasantly situated on the river aforesaid, (which abounds in plenty of fish) about one mile from the main ocean, commanding a fine prospect, and in short these works are allowed by competent judges, who have viewed the different salt works on the shore, to be equal if not superior to any in the state.

The Union Salt Works was again attacked in April 1780. Lieutenant Colonel Lawrence commanded a large and well-disciplined group of colonists loyal to the Crown who were sometimes called "the Provincials." The purpose of the attack was to capture the officers and soldiers stationed at the works to protect it. Unfavorable winds detained the expedition at Sandy Hook. In the meantime, the militia stationed at the works was transferred elsewhere. Only about six or seven men under the command of a lieutenant were left behind.

The enemy force landed at midnight on April 21,1780. They surrounded the buildings, which they thought were occupied by the militia. They sounded a bugle and ordered the Americans to surrender. Colonel Lawrence was upset that he had captured only six or seven men, but nothing could be done about it. They took their prisoners back to the ship and, some accounts say, wrecked the Union Salt Works.

The Union Salt Works faded from the public record after this event. It is not known how extensively it was wrecked in 1780 or how much of its equipment was sold in 1779.

In 1793, William Newbold died and left his estate to his five sons, including "rights in land of Squan called the Salt Works Tract held in common with Clayton Newbold." In 1812, Kaighn died and left his three-eighths interest in the Union Salt Works property to Samuel Edwards and wife.

In 1813, Samuel Edwards and wife sold the Union Salt Works lot to William Goodman of Howell. One way or another, Goodman obtained the rest of the saltworks property. In a deed on file at Freehold dated 1835, he and his wife transferred to sea captain James Henry Green (the husband of Goodman's stepdaughter Jane Leslie Green)

> *all that certain tract of land situated on the north side of Manasquan River in the township of Howell aforesaid where on the said William Goodman now dwells and known by the name of Union Salt Works lot. Beginning at a stone standing in the highway leading to Union Landing.*

This tract consisted of eleven acres.

In later years, artifacts have been found along the Brielle waterfront that may be from the Union Salt Works. Old wooden pipes were discovered at Hoffman's Anchorage, and very old bricks were found at the river's edge on properties on Green Avenue and Crescent Drive.

Standing in the area that the Union Salt Works once occupied, one can observe the Manasquan River, with its scenic beauty and interesting boating activity. Try to think back in time to what it must have been like there during the Revolution—the saltworks bustling, with wagons taking off overland and salt schooners loading at the wharf. Visualize the arrival of the British troops, the fighting that took place and the destruction of the works. It seems so peaceful at the scene now that it is hard to realize the high drama that took place there. Brielle, or Union Landing as it was known then, played an important role in the Revolutionary War.

CHAPTER 3

UNION LANDING AFTER THE REVOLUTION

Life in Union Landing from around 1783 to about 1820 was typically agrarian. The nation as a whole was getting used to the new freedom that it had recently gained. Farming was a way of life in the early days. Even a doctor, lawyer, shopkeeper or blacksmith would have at least had a small farm to take care of his family's needs. The larger farms, of course, sold their excess products. Wheat, corn, potatoes and other vegetables were grown. Apples, peaches and other fruit were abundant. Chickens and hogs were raised, and on the larger farms, cattle were also kept. Salt hay was used as feed and mulch on the farms. The abundant pine and cedar woods supplied lumber. Oxen and horses supplied the power for the plow and also for hauling the farm products.

The best method of moving all of these things to market was by coasting schooners, as the roads were at best primitive. In her book *The Brielle Story*, Helen Holmquist quotes a poem written at that time, "Wagon or Waterway":

> *The roads are not passable*
> *Not even jackass-able*
> *And those who will travel 'em*
> *Should turn out and gravel 'em.*

In dry weather, clouds of dust flew in the air as the wagons passed, and in wet weather, the wagon wheels were mired in thick mud. The old-time farmers looked forward to the winter snows to haul very heavy loads. It was much easier for the horses to pull sleds over the snow than to pull wagons over the unpaved roads.

Fishing was an important part of the lives of the people in Union Landing. The Manasquan River was alive with fish. In an early letter, a writer boasted:

There is abundance to be had everywhere through the country, in all the rivers, and the people commonly fish with long sieves or long nets, and will catch with a sieve one, sometimes two, barrels a day of good fish, which they salt up monthly, for their own use and to sell to others.

The gathering and sale of clams and oysters was also an important source of income to the residents. The long wharf at the end of Union Lane was busy with boats sailing out of the inlet to fish in the ocean. Bluefish, weakfish, striped bass, flounder, porgies and codfish were some of the kinds of fish caught.

Hunting was an added source of food for the early residents. Game included rabbits, squirrels and deer. Hunters also shot swans, geese, ducks, pigeons, quail, turkeys and other birds.

William Brown, master carpenter, owned and carried on a shipbuilding business at Union Landing. One of the many boats that he built was the *Prudence*, in 1806. It was described as being sixty-one feet, four inches long, with one deck and two masts. It was fifteen feet, four inches wide and had a depth of four feet, nine inches. It was a square-sterned and round-tucked schooner. After William Brown moved to Navesink, Captain Morris Freeman continued to build vessels at the same site until 1837.

THE WHARF AT UNION LANDING

The long wharf at Union Landing was the home port of the coastal schooners that carried farm products and lumber to New York City and other ports and returned with manufactured goods. The War of 1812 had a direct effect on the shipping from Union Landing. British warships cruised offshore, waiting for the coastal schooners to leave Manasquan Inlet. Many of the speedy little schooners outran the British brigs, but some were captured and their contents plundered.

The fate of the sailors of the captured vessels was uncertain. One captain known to have been lost in the war was Samuel Green. He was last seen heading out to sea in his schooner, being pursued by an armed British vessel. He was never heard from again. It is probable that other captains and their crews were lost or captured in this manner, but we do not know their names.

The British also fired at the shoreline, and sometimes shots fired over the bluffs struck a mile or two inland. One farm in what is now Point Pleasant had the roof of its barn hit by British shot. It is not known whether any property in Union Landing or Crabtown (later Squan Village) was hit, but it must have been nerve-wracking for the settlers to be fired at. After peace was

This painting by G.L. Bailey depicts how the landing at the foot of Union Lane would have looked in its heyday. Coasting schooners from ports to the north and south would come to Union Landing to load, unload and transfer cargo.

declared in 1815, the citizens of the area went back to their normal pursuits and the coasting trade flourished.

Monmouth Furnace was established in 1814 at the place now known as Allaire. In 1822, James P. Allaire acquired Monmouth Furnace and renamed it Howell Works. Hal Allaire, son of James P. Allaire, wrote that ironware products from this bog iron industry center were "handled by small schooners venturing in and out of the boisterous inlet, or rather outlet, of the River Manasquan."

In her booklet *Our Neighboring Village of Allaire*, Jean Kell relates:

> *Leading articles manufactured at the Howell Works were that which was known as "hollow ware"; the casting of caldrons, various sizes of pots and kettles and covered bakepans, stoves, screws, pipes and andirons. Some of the iron known as "charcoal iron" which was soft and malleable was sent to markets in bars and ingots. In the early days iron ore and its products were floated down the Manasquan River in scows, and loaded on coastwise vessels which did all the freighting out of the Manasquan Inlet.*

The long wharf at Union Landing was the home port of these coasting schooners. An early road map shows Abraham Osborn's "new" warehouse located beside this dock.

THE FIRST PUBLIC SCHOOL

Back in the late 1820s, Howell Township made the decision to place a one-room school in this "river" area of the township and chose a site near a small settlement close to the bridge, about where the Route 70 bridge is today. The first schoolmaster was Benjamin Pearce. This building burned down

The second school in the area was constructed in 1856 on the hill atop today's Schoolhouse Road by the Wall Township School Board. It was a typical rural one-room schoolhouse.

in 1840 and was rebuilt on the same site. The sole building of that era left standing in that area today is the farmhouse/tavern that is now Harpoon Willy's restaurant. The school was located nearby, not actually in today's Brielle but within a few feet of the current borough boundary. The eastern portion of Howell became Wall Township in 1851. In 1856, Wall Township built a wood clapboard, two-room school on a gravel road at the top of a hill with a view of the river and ocean. This road is today called Schoolhouse Road. This school remained in use until 1918. The materials to construct the school were purchased from Haynes Drummond & Co., Ocean Port. The total bill was $141.25. The Board of Education trustees, Elias Allen and Captain John Brown, did not pay the bill promptly. On February 10, 1858, Haynes Drummond wrote to Captain Brown requesting payment of the bill. At one time, the school was referred to locally as the "Gravel Hill Academy." It was a grammar school with one teacher. After 1918, it was moved to the Rankin farm on Rankin Road, where it was used as a barn.

One can only surmise what the settlement of Union Landing was like in these early days because very few records are left. With so many horses to be attended to, settlers must have had access to a blacksmith. The farmers must have had a mill nearby where they could take their wheat to be ground into flour. Doubtless, there was a store or two where the products brought back by the schooners were sold.

It is a shame that more is not known about the anonymous people who worked so hard without all of the modern conveniences that are a necessity today. They lived, loved, raised their children and died, leaving descendants to carry on daily life in Union Landing.

CHAPTER 4

THE COASTING TRADE

Following the Revolutionary War and the War of 1812, the country entered a period of ferment and growth. The Indian population had by that time virtually melted away in this area. This little section of Monmouth County was also not immune to, nor unaware of, the events heralding and leading to the Civil War. Union Landing was primarily an agrarian society going into this period but not an isolated community. Considerable shipping came and went from the wharf at Union Landing. A good number of sea captains and watermen resided in our area, bringing world and national news and events to the local people. The Industrial Revolution had just commenced, and by the 1870s the railroad was making plans to extend the line through Brielle and farther south. Also during this period, wealthy individuals began to notice the natural beauty of the countryside along the Manasquan River, resulting in the construction of large vacation "cottages."

Shipping and farming, the two predominant economic activities in this area, continued to grow and expand in the post–Revolutionary War era. The coasting trade was an important part of the economy along the Jersey Shore throughout the nineteenth century. Two-masted schooners and, later, three-masted vessels sailed out of the inlets along the Atlantic Coast to New York City and other ports.

Squan Inlet was particularly busy, with the home landing place at the long wharf at Union Landing. This wharf was at the end of Union Lane, which was then called Union Road. As Mrs. Lewis H. Pearce reported in her book *Squanians*:

> It was always lively around Union Landing—vessels sailing in and vessels sailing out, vessels loading and unloading. Captain Andrew Longstreet says that on one occasion he counted twenty-four schooners anchored on the river between Trunk Point and the inlet.

Trunk Point was the area along the waterfront between where the railroad is now located and Ocean Avenue.

Lumber from the surrounding pine and cedar forests and farm produce were among the principal cargoes carried by these small vessels. These early schooners drew from three to four feet of water and carried from forty to fifty tons. Later, larger vessels were built, some of which sailed directly out of New York Harbor.

Many of the captains of these schooners lived in Brielle, or Union Landing as Brielle was then called, and in other nearby communities. The Diamond Jubilee booklet *Manasquan New Jersey* states:

> *Two of the most popular young captains of these romantic days were John Maxon Brown and James Henry Green both of whom lived on the bank of the Manasquan River in two of the few houses that were situated at the water's edge.*

With growth came the need for improved communications, initially and most notably via the U.S. mail. A mail route was established between Freehold and Tuckerton on January 20, 1818. One trip per week was made from Freehold, through Squankum down the Old Bridge Road, across the Manasquan River about where Route 70 now crosses and on to Toms River, Cedar Creek, Manahawkin and Tuckerton. A post office was established near the crossing of the Manasquan River in the vicinity of the present-day historic building that houses Harpoon Willy's tavern and close to where present-day Riverview Drive meets Route 70. Samuel Allen was appointed the first postmaster.

Logs from the many pine forests bound for mills to be sawn into lumber were a typical export from this region in the 1800s. They were hauled on horse-drawn carts to the wharf, loaded onto barges and transferred to the waiting schooners.

The actual building housing that first post office was torn down about 1950, when William Blair of Point Pleasant Beach purchased the Charles Height property. In addition to the post office at this location, there was a tavern, a stagecoach stop, a school and a cider mill. In 1852, service at the post office was discontinued. The residents of Squan Village had expressed interest in having the post office moved to Squan Village; otherwise, they were compelled to travel two miles to the bridge for their mail. From 1852 until 1888, local residents were required to conduct postal business at the Squan Village office.

ROADS AND HIGHWAYS

At the height of the Federal period, which also marked the beginning of the Industrial Revolution, it became apparent that a better network of roads was needed, especially roads into the interior in Monmouth County. Early roads consisted of sand or dirt and were winding and poorly maintained, often following Indian trails. One of the first roads officially aligned and laid out in our area was Union Lane. The laying-out process involves marking and surveying the route of the road as it exists and with the proposed changes and bringing back or returning that information to the county seat, hence it was known as "return of a road" or "road return." The following is an excerpt from a "Road Return from Howell" (Brielle was part of Howell Township at the time):

We the subscribers six of the surveyors of the highways of the County of Monmouth appointed in the application of William Goodman and more than ten other Freeholders and residents of the said county by the Inferior Court of Common Pleas of the said County in the term of April last to lay out a public road of two rods wide in the Township of Howell in the said County as by the order and appointment of the said Court on the minutes of the said court, a certified copy whereof is hereunto annexed more fully appears to hereby Certify and return that having met agreeably to the order of the said Court on this twenty-seventh day of May, One thousand eight hundred and thirty three at the house of Stephen Allen innkeeper in the Township of Howell in said county and due proof being made to us that advertisements of our said meeting have been signed and setup according to law and having viewed the premises and heard what could be said for and against the road do think and adjudge the said road as applied for and as mentioned in the said orders of the Court to be necessary, and have laid out and do accordingly lay out the same as appears to us most for the public conveniency and having regard to the best ground for a road and the shortest distance in such manner as to do the least injury to private property as follows (to wit) We do lay out a public road of two rods width in the Township of Howell in the said County to begin at a stake standing in the middle of the road called Painters Road & in the line of land formerly belonging to William Longstreet dec'd being also the north line of Abraham Tysons wood lands thence south eighty two degrees and fifteen minutes east thirty six chains and twenty links to a stake standing near Richard Longstreet's upper gate by the woods being the Northwest Corner of George Rankins improved land thence south forty seven degrees & twenty minutes east fifty eight chains and thirty links to a stake standing fifty links South twenty six degrees West from the southeast corner of Abraham Osborn's new storehouse thence South forty five degrees east one chain & Sixty links to a stake thence South twenty three degrees & thirty minutes east one chain & twenty links to low water mark in Squan river at a place called the Union landing and there to end, which said lines of course are in the middle of the public road now laid out, that is to say said public road is now by us laid out at One rod in width on each side of the said lines of course hereinbefore Expressed, which said road by us laid out, we have caused to be marked at proper distances in the line of the Same, and we have caused to be made a map or draught of the said road so laid out, and of the courses and distances most remarkable places & improvements through which said road passes hereinbefore mentioned and described which map or draught is hereunto annexed, and we do hereby fix the first day of November next as the time when the overseers of the highways of the Township of Howell shall open the same for public use dated at the house of Stephen Allen the twenty eighth day of May One thousand eight hundred and thirty three.

Halsted H. Wainwright
Wm. K. VanNote
L. Edwards
Benjn. Stout
Elijah Robbins

Note that Union Lane started at Painters [*sic*] Road, which in those days ran toward the interior of the county and joined other roads leading to Freehold, branching off to the north and south. Another early road in our area is Union Avenue, which in the early days ended at Union Lane. Riverview Drive did not come into existence until the twentieth century. Higgins Avenue, first known as Bridge Avenue, did not come into existence until 1872, when a bridge was constructed at the eastern end of the Manasquan River. In the early part of this period, Ocean County did not exist—it was part of Monmouth County. The two counties did not split until 1850. The portion of the county south of the

Manasquan River could only be reached by boat until 1816, when a wooden bridge known as the "Squan long bridge" was built over the river, about where the current-day Route 70 bridge is located. In 1830, that bridge was replaced by a wooden swing bridge, which remained in service for over one hundred years. A bridge at this site facilitated mail service to the southern portion of Monmouth County. Until the 1870s, this was the only local bridge across the river.

THE MANASQUAN RIVER AND THE SHIPPING TRADE

The Manasquan River is one of the defining and important aspects of local geography and history, especially in the time period between 1820 and 1880. The river provided food, was a means of transportation and was one of the early attractions that brought what would become a vital commodity in later years—tourists.

Over the years, the inlet itself silted up, often after storms. In the 1820s, the inlet was almost two miles farther north of its present location and came down parallel to the coast, creating a barrier island in present-day Sea Girt and Manasquan. By 1868, the opening to the sea had migrated south over a mile, and it had moved even farther by the 1870s. By 1879, the inlet was near its present location but continued to be subject to variations in position and depth, according to the tides and weather conditions.

Shallow draft vessels could navigate this waterway, making Union Landing a busy seaport. A long wharf was built out into the river for commercial and pleasure use. William Brown, who began building vessels at Union Landing in 1808, moved to Navesink a few years later. Captain Morris Freeman, who continued at the same site, succeeded him. Also in this area on the north shore of the river were Captain Shem Pearce, Curtis & Pearce, Captain Hartshorn Jackson, A. and Nesbit Hanaway, Jacob Herbert, Corlis L. Cooper and David Newbury. Some continued boat building or shipbuilding as individuals, in partnership arrangements or alliances that altered over a period of years, in various different locations or in other combinations that may have changed in other ways over time.

The names of the vessels built on the river were recorded in the annual *Registry of Merchant Vessels* or in similar volumes. New "registry certificates" were executed when a vessel's ownership was changed by reason of sale or partnership, recording the names of all owners, the ship's master and occasionally further information. Vessels able to negotiate the shallow entrance to our river had to be shoal draft, most being constructed with a centerboard, which was needed to provide the additional lateral plane so that they could sail to windward without

Left: This wooden bridge was constructed in 1830 across the Manasquan River at Old Bridge Road. Until the 1870s, this was the only bridge across the river in this area. The bridge remained in service for over one hundred years.

Below: This early map of the inlet mouth shows it at a position near its present location. In those days, the currents and weather often formed a barrier island that ran north and south between the river and the open ocean.

tipping over. The depth of a vessel would vary from 3.5 feet to about 5 feet. Schooners built here included the *Allen Osborn*, length of 59.3 feet, built in 1864; Captain Thomas Tilton's *Columbian*, length 59 feet, built in 1849; Captain Billy Jackson's *Breeze*, length 57.8 feet, built in 1877; and Captain James Green's *Glide*, length 41.8 feet, built in 1855. An example of a sloop built on the river was the *Jennie Arnold*, length 28.2 feet, built in 1876.

Cargo carried from Union Landing for sale in larger urban markets included local products such as boards, cedar rails, plastering lath, cedar pickets, hoop poles, charcoal, clams, oysters, crabs, eels and other fish from the river, as well as fruits and vegetables. The return cargo consisted of manufactured goods, which were not produced locally. During the nineteenth century, a prosperous industry developed here, shipping large quantities of these items mainly to New York. The advent of the railroad in the last quarter of the nineteenth century spelled the end of ship carriage from Union Landing.

UNION LANDING–BASED SEA CAPTAINS

The sailing vessels built in the early years for service in the coastal trade out of Union Landing were primarily sloops and two-masted schooners, forty to fifty tons and drawing between three and four feet of water. The hull frames were constructed of local white oak, with other materials brought in. However, one vessel, the *Enterprise*, was known to have been entirely built from various types of hand-hewn southern Monmouth County wood.

The following table provides some information on those early mariners (see "Notes" following this list):

NAME	BORN	DIED	VESSELS COMMANDED	NOTES
Bailey, Forman O.	Aug. 10, 1843	1930	SS *Thorp*, *Henry S. Little*	1
Bailey, George G.	Nov. 11, 1839	Jan. 6, 1916	*William H. Bailey*	2
Bailey, Henry	May 14, 1845	Oct. 18, 1874	*Thomas R. Woolley*	3
Bailey, John	1841	1868	*C.H. Malison*, *Ida Grant*	4
Bailey, Marvin	1874	1908	*William H. Bailey*, *Charles G. Endicott*	5
Bailey, William Henry	Jan. 15, 1815	Dec. 1, 1899	*Abram Osborn*	6
Bennett, Stewart	1835		*Gracie D. Chambers*	
Brannin, James	Sept. 11, 1810	Aug. 20, 1899	*Wave*, *Mary Jane*	
Brown, George	1831		*Sinepuxent*	
Brown, John Ashley				7
Brown, Joseph Hanley			*Fiorella*	
Brown, John M.	Jun. 1, 1808	Nov. 13, 1896	*Pinta*	8

Name	Born	Died	Vessels Commanded	Notes
Brown, Lucien	1849		*John K. Shaw*	9
Brown, Morris	Oct. 1, 1811	Jul. 2, 1892	*Enterprise*	
Brown, Theodore S.P.	1841		*O.H. Brown, Charles Woolsey*	
Clark, William	1811	1880	*Breeze*	
Craig, James	1833			
Curtis, Abraham	1842	1899	*John B. Spofford*	
Curtis, Asa	1848			
Curtis, Asher	1849	Jan. 2, 1929	*Charles H. Valentine, George Bailey, Sarah W. Lawrence*	
Curtis, James	1820 (?)		*John T. Young, William A. Brooks, James K. Polk, Liberty*	
Curtis, John	Jan. 17, 1851	Aug. 28, 1897	*Bertha Walker*	
Curtis, Lewis	1827			
Curtis, Pitney	Nov. 19, 1825	Aug. 5, 1889	*John T. Williams*	10
Curtis, Pitney E.	Nov. 15, 1859	Oct. 4, 1877		
Curtis, Tylie			*Thomas A. Ward*	11
Curtis, Vaden	1853		*I.J. Merritt, King, Valentine*	
Freeman, Morris	1789			12
Green, Edward			*Gracie D. Chambers*	
Green, James Edward	1844	1896	*William Clark*	13
Green, James H. (Captain Jim)	1825			
Green, James Henry	1808	Jan. 2, 1878	*Banner, Bound, Glide*	14
Green, William Henry	Sept. 25, 1841	Apr. 24, 1911	*Rhoda Holmes, Charles Noble Simmons, Sunlight*	
Hudson, Perry	Oct. 11, 1828	Jul. 26, 1907	*Alice Pearce*	
Jackson, Billy	Sept. 2, 1821(?)	Feb. 25, 1893(?)	*Columbian*	
Jackson, Hart			*Fourth of July*	15

Name	Born	Died	Vessels Commanded	Notes
Longstreet, Abram			*T. Lupton, J.W. Morris, Charles Woolsey*	
Longstreet, Andrew J.	1834	Oct. 28, 1926	*John E. Clayton*	16
Longstreet, Cornelius	Feb. 16, 1809	Feb. 6, 1888	*Elizabeth, Triton*	
Longstreet, Enos	Jul. 15, 1850	Feb. 10, 1918		17
Longstreet, Jake (Jacob?)	1810		*Banner*	
Longstreet, James	Jul. 5, 1818	Dec. 18, 1902		
Longstreet, James J.	1826			
Longstreet, Jimmy O.			*Manna*	
Longstreet, Randolph	1846		*Greenleaf Johnson*	18
Longstreet, Spencer	1857(?)	Oct. 9, 1894	*John D. Williams*	19
Longstreet, Stout			*Breeze*	
Longstreet, Tabor	Aug. 22, 1822	1893	*James W.*	
Lyman (Liming), Benjamin	Jun. 1, 1825	Dec. 19, 1905	*Thomas A. Ward*	
Lyman, Pitney C.	Sept. 13, 1861	Jul. 28, 1892		
Osborn, Benjamin			*The Native*	
Osborn, Lucien	1849	1884	*John K. Shaw*	20
Osborn, Marion			*Marjorie Brown, Keinberg*	
Pearce, Alvin	Nov. 18, 1873	Nov. 9, 1934	*Augusta, Francis Taussig, Esther K.*	
Pearce, Ambrose	1850			
Pearce, Archie	Jan. 29, 1872	Jun. 15, 1914	*Job H. Jackson, Henry S. Little*	
Pearce, Cohen Sora	Feb. 10, 1861	Dec. 5, 1942	SS *Thorp*	21
Pearce, David	1848		*Thomas L. James*	
Pearce, Edgar L.	Dec. 24, 1896		*Calvin B. Orcutt*	22
Pearce, Edward	1838			
Pearce, Edwin L.	May 22, 1839	Jan. 13, 1899	*Benjamin Van Brunt*	
Pearce, Ernest	Feb. 1942		*Sintram*	23
Pearce, George				
Pearce, Joseph T.	May 10, 1819	May 17, 1869	*The Vineyard*	

NAME	BORN	DIED	VESSELS COMMANDED	NOTES
Pearce, Lewis E.	Aug. 14, 1826	Feb. 7, 1908	*F. Merwin, Mattie V. Rulon, Lookout, American, Irene*	
Pearce, Lewis H.	Nov. 10, 1851	Jan. 14, 1930	*Samuel S. Thorpe, Nellie W. Craig, Henry Sutton, Jeanie C. May, Charles A. Campbell*	
Pearce, Oscar	Mar. 10, 1863	Oct. 13–16, 1889	*John S. Hasbrook, Nellie W. Craig*	24
Pearce, W. Irving	Feb. 15, 1863	Jun. 16, 1942	*Malcom Baxter Jr., Henry S. Little*	
Pearce, Wynant V.	Jun. 8, 1822	Jun. 28, 1905	*John D. Williams*	
Poland, Cornelius	Dec. 8, 1827	Mar. 24, 1917	*Stranger, Farewell*	
Rankin, George	1835		*Enterprise*	
Rankin, James E.			*Eliza Jane*	25
Rogers, John S.	Aug. 4, 1817	Aug. 26, 1890	*Breeze, Fashion, White Oak*	
Simon, Benjamin	1836			
Simon, Elwood	1859		*captain of a schooner (1880 Census)*	
Thompson, Abram			*Marjorie Brown, P.C. Schultz*	
Thompson, James	Mar. 3, 1823	Jun.23, 1885	*Peter C. Schultz*	
Thompson, Stephen			*Charles H. Valentine*	
Tilton, Edward	1837		*Adelaide Barbour*	
Tilton, George	1852		*Maggie M. Keough, Viking*	
Tilton, Thomas L.	Sept. 21, 1816	Jul. 28, 1880	*Riley Allen, Faithful Friend, Abram Osborn, Briton M. Tilton*	

Notes

1. Forman O. Bailey was a son of William H. Bailey. He went to sea at age twelve. At age twenty, he was master of a ship. In later years, he owned six three-masted vessels and four four-masted vessels. He also owned considerable Manasquan real estate and was an early promoter of the First National Bank of Manasquan. He defended coastal shipping captains in a letter to a New York City newspaper on March 26, 1886, stating:

As a class they are the most practical and thoroughbred seamen that go down to the sea in ships. Seventy five percent of them learn their trade by beginning in small boats and by degrees work themselves up and through experience become quite capable of their charge.

2. George Bailey went to sea at age eighteen and sailed for twenty-six years. He sailed the three-masted *William H. Bailey*, named for his father. He owned the *Calvin B. Orcutt* and was managing owner of the *Henry S. Little*. He never had a serious accident at sea.

3. Henry Bailey died at age twenty-nine years, five months and three days.

4. John Bailey was a son of William H. Bailey.

5. Marvin Bailey was swept off the deck of the *Charles G. Endicott* near Bodie Island, North Carolina, and was never found.

6. William Henry Bailey retired from the sea in 1866. His sons were Forman Osborn, George, Henry and John.

7. John Ashley Brown was lost at sea.

8. John M. Brown served as a sea captain during the Mexican War. He later engaged in business as the proprietor of the Union House at Union Landing. He was awarded the Life-Saving Association gold medal for aiding in the rescue of persons from the shipwrecked *John Farnum*, *Cornelius Grinnell*, *New Era*, *New York* and *Western World*. His father, William Brown, was a shipbuilder at Union Landing.

9. Captain Lucien Brown went down with the *John K. Shaw*.

10. Pitney Curtis was captain of the *Alice L. Pierce*, which was wrecked on November 23, 1876. He and a crew of three were saved.

11. Captain Tylie Curtis's ship was lost on December 9, 1917, off the Florida coast. He and eight men arrived safely in New York City on December 14, 1917.

12. Morris Freeman was listed in the census as a shipwright.

13. James Edward and William Henry Green were the sons of James Henry Green.

14. James Henry Green lived on the Manasquan River.

15. Hart Jackson was also a boat builder on the north side of the Manasquan River.

16. Andrew J. Longstreet was considered the youngest local sea captain. When he was only nineteen years of age, he contracted for the ship *John H. Clayton* to be built. He died at age ninety-two.

17. Captain Enos Longstreet was a son of Captain James A. Longstreet.

18. Captain Randolph Longstreet was another son of Captain James A. Longstreet.

19. At age thirty-seven, Spencer Longstreet, son of Captain James A. Longstreet, went down with the *John D. Williams*. All hands were lost.

20. Lucien Osborn was lost at sea.

21. Captain Cohen Pearce remained a bachelor. He was a son of Lewis E. Pearce. In 1915, a steamer in Long Island Sound struck his ship, the SS *Thorp*. It was towed into New London, where repairs were made.

22. Edgar L. Pearce, another son of Lewis E. Pearce, was captain of the four-masted *Calvin B. Orcutt*. This vessel went aground off Chatham, Massachusetts, on Christmas Eve 1896 in a blinding snowstorm and gale. All nine aboard lost their lives. Pieces of the ship were found to identify this tragedy.

23. A steamship ran into the *Sintram* and the ship began to sink. It is stated that Captain Ernest Pearce returned to the sinking ship to rescue the ship's cat and clock. It is said that the clock remained in the family.

24. Oscar Pearce, another son of Lewis E. Pearce, went down with the *John L. Hasbrook*. All hands were lost.

25. James Rankin was captain of the *Eliza Jane*, with two masts and a flying jib. The ship sank on September 2, 1876. The crew of six was saved.

CAPTAIN JOHN M. BROWN

Captain John Maxon Brown was born in 1808 at Union Landing, where his father, William, was a leading shipbuilder. The Brown farm was a very large property that extended from the riverfront along the south side of Union Lane. Their cow pasture is now Greenwood Cemetery. His parents moved to Navesink, where he spent his childhood, and in 1829 he first went to sea, later serving as a captain for many years. Captain Brown was a family man and as such would write to his wife and family from the various ports where his travels brought him. Following is a letter written by Captain Brown while in port at Philadelphia. While it may not be considered far away today, back then it was at least a few days' journey from Union Landing. Being a businessman and master of a sailing vessel, he would have had to be literate, but as the reader will see, his skills were not quite at today's standards. He writes:

Philadelpa Janury the 10 1847

Dear wife i take this Sundy evning to Rite you as folars that i am well And hope that tis will find you the Same and all of the children; Dear wife i had Dispach the i expected wen I rote you Last I finished Last nite a Bout 7 oclock and shal Leav on mondy after I clear the vessel out from the custom house and sine my Charterparty i had rote John moreau if there comes a Leter from you to Late to reach me for to send it Back to you i Am Bound to Brases Santago at a ----- Charter of 1800 Dolars and 30 Dolars a Day after 5 Days Laing ther if not on Lodid in that time if i am onlodid i shal Lode the Vesel some Place close By for home i will rite you every opertunity after this after i finish this i shal rite one to John A. Brown Dear mary i

*cant Say now or then for you to Do as you think Best a Bout the Property til
i come home in the spring if you can sel the horses for 230 Dolars or 200
hundred Dolars you may sel them if you please or any thing you pleas*

*Mary Dear i give you up every thing to Doe As you pleas sell and Doe as
you pleas and I Will Be sadisfied Only Bleave that I Am Doeing the Best I can
Bleave for you And our children I know that it is not for My one comfort that
I am not home a talking With you in stid of riting to you My Dear the Lord
Noes our harts and noes that i am not taking comfort for my Self But for a home
for you and My children wich i had Ben the case of Bringin in the would Dear
Wife it makes mee shudder to think that you or they should want for Bread or
a home i would Bee wiling to Sufer more then i even had rether then that Shold
happen my Dear the Lord has Bin mercieful to wardes mee On you a count for
i feele that your Prares has kept mee ware i am Dear mary remember mee to the
Lord every morning and nite i think of you every ouer in the Day i Do Bleav
My Dear Don't get discourage But put your trust in the Lord and Bleave that
your Prares will Be herd Dear mary Bleave mee you are the only hope that i had
i mest stop i remane yours wilest Life Last John M. Brown*
give my love to all of my children

His abilities attracted the attention of the board of directors of the Coast
Wrecking Company, and for forty years he held the position of wreckmaster
in that dangerous service, until 1873. A special gold medal was struck by the
company in recognition of his meritorious service that reads:

Captain John M. Brown as he appeared
later in life. This photograph was taken
after he retired from the sea and his
service as wreckmaster. He was the
proprietor of the Union House.

This gold-plated medal was awarded to Captain John M. Brown by the Life-Saving Benevolent Association to recognize Brown's service as wreckmaster. During his tenure as wreckmaster, Brown saved many lives and salvaged a considerable amount of equipment and cargo, much to the benefit of the insurance companies.

Presented April 1857 to John M. Brown of Squan, New Jersey for his humane & Christian efforts in saving the crew & passengers of the NEWERA/ CORNELIAUS GRINNELL and other vessels wrecked on the shores of New Jersey.

Note that at the time Captain Brown was recognized as a resident of Squan, New Jersey, though his residence was in what is known today as Brielle. At that time, Manasquan was still a part of Wall Township as well.

Captain Brown's sons were also seamen, and two of them were lost at sea.

Later in life, he converted the family homestead into the Union House, a riverside hotel at the foot of Union Lane, which he managed for many years. He married Mary Pearce on January 8, 1830, and they were married for sixty-six years, until Brown's death. He spent his latter years at a cottage nearby and died on November 10, 1896. Brown's daughter Adelaide married Henry Wainwright, and they continued to operate the hotel after Brown retired. The building burned down in 1914.

CAPTAIN JAMES HENRY GREEN

Captain James Henry Green was born in 1808. His father, Samuel, was also a sea captain and was lost at sea off Squan Inlet during the War of 1812. He was observed heading out to sea in his small schooner, being pursued by an armed British vessel. He was not heard from again. Captain James Henry Green, or "Captain Henry" as he was usually called, owned and sailed three schooners. In 1829, Captain Henry married Sarah Jane Adelaide Leslie, and they settled down on their property on the Manasquan River. They owned all the land from Union Lane along what is today Green Avenue to current Homestead Road to Longstreet Creek, thence back to the river at Union Lane. This area was known then as "Green's Point." Today, that area includes Green Avenue, named after

Captain Henry; Homestead Road; Leslie Avenue, named after Jane Leslie Green; Manasquan Avenue; Lake Avenue; and the area that later became Crescent Drive and Ocean Avenue. Captain Henry and his wife had two sons and six daughters. The two sons, William Henry and James Edward, both became sea captains. Three of their six daughters married sea captains. Caroline Elizabeth married Captain Lewis Ellison Pearce, Julia Matilda married Captain Pitney Curtis and Sarah Jane Adelaide married Captain Abraham O. Curtis.

A NATION DIVIDED: THE CIVIL WAR

Former Union Landing Historical Society president Pete Neary wrote in *Union Landing Revisited*:

> *In the spring of 1861, Brielle was then a part of Wall Township. Every day, along the sandy roads horses and wagons carried merchandise and other sundries from village to village. In the back of one wagon, securely tied, were bundles of newspapers,* The Freehold Democrat, *published at the county seat, some 17 miles up the Squan Turnpike. This paper as far as can be determined was the only means of written communication and information in this area, other than gossip and rumor passed from neighbor to neighbor. It must have been a time of great anxiety on the banks of the Manasquan. War was in the air. The Southern states have been threatening secession—a withdrawal from the Union. So on this spring day in April—to be precise, on the 18ᵗʰ of April 1861, the* Democrat *was eagerly scanned, and there in relatively modest headlines, in the middle of the front page was the opening line, in the understated journalistic style of the day: "The Ball is Opened" and a sub-title—"The War Commenced; Fort Sumter Fired Upon at Four O'clock this Morning." The local populace was shocked and distressed. We are sure thoughts of spring plowing, work at the river, etc. were put aside for the moment as they read further. President Lincoln had immediately requisitioned four New Jersey Regiments of 720 men each of which would be assigned to a Division of the state. The third division included Monmouth County. In each county were to be fifteen to twenty organized companies. A number of young men in our area hurried to join in the defense of the Union. In the April 25ᵗʰ edition of the* Democrat *specific note is made of young men from our area: "the boys have caught the war fever, and a troop of them paraded yesterday and marched through the streets, with a drum, hurrahing, and keeping admirable step to the music." There is no community memorial for those watermen and farm boys who marched away to the drummer's beat. Some came back to farm and fish, and some did not return, ever.*

A young man named James Gardner was one such soldier. James lived with his wife, Ann, and two children in the vicinity of Captain John Brown's Union House at the end of Union Lane. Gardner enlisted in September 1862 in Company K of the Twenty-ninth Infantry Regiment, New Jersey. By October 1962, his regiment began marching south toward Washington, D.C., and Virginia. While on the long journey south, Gardner found time to write to his friend Captain Brown back in Union Landing:

Letter
Camp Monmouth
Near fort mclllen octer 10 1862

Capt Brown Dear Sir
I take this oppertunity of Writing to you to inform you of my were abouts and how I am getting along. With my soldiering businefs down hear in Dixie.
I like it very much some times it comes kind tight. But I must expect some hard times in War, as I wrote to Eliz. Last We were to capitol hill that day about 3 O'clock P.M. We were ordered to pack up our furniture and kitchen utentiels and start from some place unknown to me until I reached it. We started abot 3 o'clock P.M. Went through Washing to White house and from thence through george town the moon shone as brite as day the cornal halted up several times during the march, wich was about seven mils. We Reached tenly about 10 o'clock that night. We camped on the ground with nothing but heaven for a cover and it was the same Monday night. Tuesday we got our tents. Now we are comfortable situated near fort mclellen. We are to work on the fort or rifle pits where we will be likely to stay for some time. I think Capt. Will you please to send me 23 cents worth of Postage stamps to mail my letters for they are very Scarce hear. Give my love to my whife and family and to all of my friends.
The 14th I cannot find out where they ar if you can find out Where they ar, Will you please send me word of their Werebouts.

Please write soon nomore at Present
But I Remain, ect.
James Gardner

It is not known what action, if any, Gardner saw during the war. He returned safely to Squan and mustered out of K Company on June 3, 1863, in Freehold, New Jersey.

Being drafted into the army was not always what you would imagine. Young men of privilege or wealth were able to send a substitute into the

Local resident Henry Osborn presented this certificate of exemption to his Civil War draft board to document the fact that he had furnished a substitute to complete his military obligation.

During the Civil War, firms such as Valentine & McDonald profited by contracting and furnishing substitute soldiers for those who could afford to hire them.

service in their place. In fact, a thriving business arose to fulfill this very need for those who were wealthy enough to afford it. One local boy, Henry Osborn, when drafted, was able to secure a substitute to complete his military service in the war.

The year 1880 marked the death of local resident Colonel James P. Osborn. Son of Revolutionary War veteran Lieutenant Abraham Osborn, in his eighty-three years James outlived his three wives and several of his children. Though he lived to a very old age for the day, he was, in his later years, blind and in some degree of infirmity. No one, though, is truly sure of exactly how infirm or clearheaded he was. Upon his death, he left a sizeable estate of property southwest of the present Manasquan River Golf Club. The terms of his will were not to the liking of many of his offspring. With a family of stepsiblings with three different mothers, there were bound to be differences of opinion between them. Catherine E. Collins and some of her siblings contested the colonel's last will and testament, fighting for what they deemed a "fairer" share of the estate. Though he had many children, they did not appear to get along, and any accusations between them were primarily one-sided, since they rarely associated with one another. The essence of the case was a group of dissatisfied offspring who felt cheated by their father's will, despite the fact that all of them felt that they had treated their father well in his last days. Similarly, they all felt that they had done their part to care for the ailing man. When the case was brought before the court, many witnesses were called to testify on behalf of one sibling or another to help substantiate each claimant's story of how they had conducted themselves toward their father. Osborn's lawyer, who drew up and later revised the will, was also a key witness. The trial was held in Freehold, the county seat, at a distance of some nineteen miles from the late colonel's last residence. At the time of the proceedings, that was a considerable distance to travel—several hours' journey on the roads of the day. The magnitude of the trial and the number of witnesses called to testify made it into what could only be described in today's terms as a media circus. It was literally the talk of the town, since everyone in the area at least knew someone involved if they weren't a witness themselves.

THOMAS LAWS

Thomas Laws was born in 1867 in Gloucester County, Virginia. Thomas was the youngest of ten children and as a small boy loved to play at the docks where coasting schooners made port. Thomas was an eager and helpful boy who frequently ran errands for the ship captains. He became especially friendly with Captain Osborn of Manasquan, New Jersey. When he was ten, Thomas's mother died, leaving his father alone to care for him and his siblings. Captain Osborn's friend Captain Forman O. Bailey was at that time in need of a servant to help his wife back in Manasquan. Osborn presented to Thomas's father the idea of bringing Thomas back to Manasquan to work for the Baileys. His father consented, and in 1877 young Thomas left Virginia on an oyster boat bound for Manasquan. Thomas was an industrious boy and a great help around the house to Mrs. Bailey, but he was also one of the first blacks to live in this area and as such was not received so well by many. Other children taunted him and threw rocks and eggs at him in the streets. Thomas was eager to learn but was not permitted to attend school because he was black. Mrs. Bailey taught Thomas to read and write his name, but that was the extent of his formal education. Years later, when Thomas married, Captain Bailey helped him to purchase a piece of property where he could build a house for himself and his bride. Thus, in 1890 Thomas Laws became the first black landowner in the Brielle-Manasquan area.

CHAPTER 5

REAL ESTATE DEVELOPMENT AND THE RISE OF TOURISM

The years between 1850 and 1919 brought many changes to Union Landing. In 1850, a resort industry began to take root with the opening of Captain John M. Brown's Union House at the foot of Union Lane on the river. The following article, published in the July 17, 1877 issue of the *Seaside* and titled "An Advantage," summed up the charms of our riverside area:

> *We address this article to those who really mean to have a good time somewhere this summer, to those who want some rest, some fun and hope to get back in the fall, new men and women. Now one of the advantages of Squan and vicinity over Long Branch or Newport or such places is the magnificent water of the "broad Manasquan" river. At either of the last mentioned places the stock in trade consists mainly in hops, balls, bathing and driving. While these are all very well in their way, yet there is oftentimes so much fiss and sizz and sputter about them that they are robbed of their beneficial effects. What people really need is freedom, the sense of liberty and the opportunity to metaphorically jump up and crack their heels together. We claim, then, that the Manasquan River will give anyone what he wants in this direction. Here is yachting and fishing and crabbing to the heart's content. Here may be seen anytime guests of the different houses rowing and catching crabs and having a good time generally. No one but an experienced seaman wants to sail or fish on the old ocean and the river affords an opportunity for people to go out where they please, stay as long as they please and be the captains of their own crafts. If you intend to come to the seaside for permanent good, we ask if it isn't better to come to Squan where you can have not only balls, hops, drives and ocean bathing but also sailing, fishing, and crabbing on a broad body of water, feeling all the time that you are perfectly secure, than it is to go to a place where you are denied these and can never go out on the water with out having an old sea-dog along to keep you from falling overboard and pull you out if you should happen to?*

JUNE 29, 1888.

CRESTDALE SCRIBBLINGS.

The "Jennie Arnold" is launched, and is hard to beat in the yacht line.

Mr. W. H. Wiley's family are cosily established at Osprey Bluff.

The storm of Wednesday night has swollen the streams and flooded the earth.

The intense heat of the past w_ _k has given place to a comfortable te - perature once more.

Mrs. C. V. Sanborn, the artist, is busy with her class amid the natural beauties of the section.

Little Miss Florence Hutchinson of Crestdale Villa, caught a mess of eels, her first lesson from Sir. Izaak Walton.

Mr. Bart Pearce, the boat architect, is now being assisted by Mr. John Pearce and Captain Louis Curtis, of Union Lane.

Gay equipages from the villages above and below may be seen daily bowling along the shore, taking in the beauties of land and sea.

Mr. George Butts is at the Union House. Messrs. Will Hart, Theo. Butts and Louis Benson, so well and favorably known along the shore, were down last Sunday.

The Season of '88 is fairly opened at the Carteret, and promises to be very successful. About fifty guests are due this week and applications are daily made for accommodations. In fact, at the present rate, an addition will have to be built to the hotel. Prof. Kramer, with his orchestra, so popular already among our citizens, will furnish music during the season, which will open with a grand hop on the 4th of July. A stage, free of charge will run to the seashore, and once a week the yacht, hired by the proprietor of the Carteret, will be at the service of his guests. The time is not far distant when the Carteret will rival all other seaside resorts. The register shows the following guests :— From Jersey City, Mr. and Mrs. E. Whyte, Mr. and Mrs. Jos. Bets, Miss Von Bamberger and Mrs. C. Schraedu and daughter. From Hoboken, Mr. and Mrs. Kemble, Mr. and Mrs. Feldstein and daughter, Mr. and Mrs. W. Lierck and family. From Brooklyn, Mr. and Mrs. Prentiss from New York, Mr. and Mrs. Perry.

Mrs. Richardson was the proud owner of a pig. Not a stuck pig, or a trained pig, or a roast pig. Just a live pig, whose comfortable proport'ons she had measured and calculated as to future usefulness in the culinary line. A pig with one ear slit and the other ear cropped, but with the usual complement of nose, eyes, feet, hide and tail. A spotted pig, in fact, of no mean pretentions. He was trusted in full with the limits of the grounds, and was educated to stop at home, quietly or squeakily, just as he pleased. Now, to show the value of early training where the spirit is restless and the morals are easy, his pigship helped himself to a hearty supper— very hearty—and then disappeared. Fled from his own vine and fig tree and swill trough to unknown seas. He was traced to the river bank where he took a boat for some strange port, whether foreign or native history sayeth not. But he was careful not to get muddy for, sad to tell, he purloined a pair of rubber boots and left plain tracks in the sand. He also had a sharp tussel with some other emigrating pig, (perhaps) for there were marks all about of a struggle. But Mrs Richards' pig, like Mrs. O' Leary's cow, came off triumphant and escaped. E.

The *Seaside* newspaper, forerunner of today's *Coast Star*, would publish weekly reports of society doings in local hotels and towns.

Many of the local goings-on and rosters of the notable guests who had lodged at local hotels for the season were published in the local newspaper, the *Seaside*, in a sort of society column. The *Seaside* is still published today as the *Coast Star*.

Tad Dalrymple on the banks of the Manasquan River about 1900. The bridge in the background was the first auto bridge across the eastern end of the river.

THE RAILROAD COMES TO BRIELLE

A major catalyst for change was the coming of the railroad to the shore area. In 1872, the iron horse arrived in Squan Village on a single-track line that crossed Broad Street and proceeded north to Sea Girt. The easternmost part of this line was built by the Farmingdale and Squan Village Railroad Company. As was typical in the day, small sections of a continuous run of track were owned and operated by different railroad companies. By 1879, after several railroad company mergers, including the Jamesburg & Freehold Agricultural Railroad, a continuous line existed from Squan Village to the Camden and Amboy line at Jamesburg and on to Philadelphia. A station for this line was subsequently built by the Pennsylvania Railroad Company on Broad Street to accommodate the travelers. Remnants of this line remain visible today in the form of the Edgar Felix bicycle path that occupies the old railroad right of way extending from the borough of Manasquan westward to the Manasquan Reservoir.

The New York and Long Branch line reached Squan Village in 1880. In November of that year, a train station was moved from Sea Plain (North Spring Lake) to a new location next to Main Street. The first railroad bridge over the Manasquan River was completed in June 1880, enabling the line to extend its reach farther south to Bay Head. It would continue south to Seaside and from there westward all the way to Toms River. In January 1882, the Jersey Central and Pennsylvania Railroads reached an agreement that both companies would use the New York and Long Branch line.

The telegraph had been invented by Samuel F.B. Morse in 1837 and was often brought into a region with the development of railroads. The railroad was operating in this area for some time before the telegraph arrived here. The railroad right of way was an obvious place for the telegraph lines to be placed. The telegraph office was located in the railroad station, and the railroad agent was usually the telegraph operator. The local telegraph office here was in the Manasquan station. This office handled telegrams for Manasquan, Union Landing (Brielle) and Point Pleasant. Before the telephone arrived, the agent sent messengers to deliver the telegrams. They travelled by horseback, wagon or boat on their appointed rounds in all kinds of weather. The messenger who had to deliver to Point Pleasant either had to go to Union Landing and get a boat to row across the river or go all the way up to the bridge at what is now Route 70. It must have been a relief to him when the railroad bridge crossed the river from Union Landing to Point Pleasant in 1880—the road bridge at what is now Route 35 was built at about the same time.

The railroads flourished in both passenger and freight service. The increasing carrying of freight brought about the demise of the coasting trade in this area. It eventually faded away, and the little coasting schooners no longer carried cargo on a regular basis. This changed the entire economy of Union Landing. Some of the larger three- and four-masted schooners continued to carry bulk cargo, such as coal and lumber. These vessels were often moored in the larger ports like Perth Amboy and South Amboy.

EARLY HOTELS AND RESORTS IN BRIELLE

As word of Brielle's natural beauty and favorable location began to spread, it became a popular vacation and resort destination. As was the case in those days, only the wealthy could afford to travel great distances to vacation. Because of the time and trouble involved in traveling, vacations often lasted for weeks at a time or even for an entire season, if one could afford it.

Real Estate Development and the Rise of Tourism

One of the earliest hotels in the area was the house known as Tippecanoe-on-Manasquan, which was built originally as a hunting and fishing lodge. Prior to his election as the ninth president of the United States in 1840, William Henry Harrison visited there. Harrison earned the nickname "Old Tippecanoe" in 1811 after his sweeping victory over Tecumseh and the Shawnees at the Battle of Tippecanoe in the Indiana Territory. Harrison was hailed as a hero following the battle but was also allegedly the recipient of a curse by Tecumseh's brother, Tenskwatawa. Popularly known as Tecumseh's curse, it forecasts that any president elected in a year ending in zero will die in office. Elected in 1840, Harrison died one month after his inauguration in April 1841. The proprietor of the lodge changed the name to Tippecanoe Farm after Harrison's visit, presumably in an attempt to attract customers. George Risley, one of the other early owners of the property, attempted to construct a swimming pool at the riverbank behind the house. Risley's swimming pool was little more than a system of free-standing bulkheads that, through openings to the river, would change its water twice daily with

An early interior view of the Tippecanoe-on-Manasquan hunting lodge. Though moved back from its original site on the river and expanded in later years, the log cabin styling is still visible.

Tippecanoe-on-Manasquan as it appeared on the riverfront. Note the windmill of the type that dotted the Brielle landscape in early years. The windmills powered pumps that drew drinking water from the aquifers beneath Brielle's soil.

Union House, Brielle, N. J.

An early view of the Union House Hotel as it would have appeared to Robert Louis Stevenson and other guests in the late nineteenth century.

the tides. The project was never sucessfully completed. Later, in the 1920s, this house was moved away from the riverbank to the corner of Riverview Drive and Isham Circle, where it still stands.

Some of the captains of the schooners used the money that they had made in the coasting trade to build hotels and boardinghouses to serve the needs of the increasing number of visitors to the area. Captain John Maxon Brown's Union House is one such example. Captain Brown's daughter Adelaide and her husband, Henry Wainwright, managed the Union House in later years. The Wainwrights ran a store in connection with the Union House, and the first telephone in town was installed there. The store also served as the post office, which was established there in 1888. Mr. Wainwright was the first postmaster, and when he died in 1911, his son Stanley became postmaster. In 1910, a group of volunteers established the Brielle Fire Company at a meeting in this general store. Doubtless, other organizations also used the building as a meeting place. The Union House and the store burned down in 1914.

Wainwright's General Store on Union Lane as it appeared in about 1903. A prominent business and meeting place, the store was also home to the borough's first telephone. Note the Bell System sign on the post.

BRIELLE

Captain Wynant V. Pearce purchased some land next to the Union House from Captain Brown and built the Crestdale House in 1877 as a private residence. Later, the house was expanded into a hotel known as the Crestdale, which was very popular, not only with visitors to Union Landing, but also with the locals who went to the dances held there on Saturday nights. This hotel was located on the riverfront where the Brielle Landing condominiums are now located. Unfortunately, the building later burned down.

Captain Dory Brown built Brown's Inn in the late 1800s. It was a large place located on the riverfront near the end of Brown Street, next to the present Bogan's Brielle Basin. This hotel also burned down.

The Andrew J. Scheible house was a large boardinghouse called the Windemere. It was originally on the riverfront where Bogan's Brielle Basin now stands. Before the new Route 35 bridge was completed in 1950, the old house was turned around and moved to its new location on Ashley Avenue, next to the present Brielle Bait and Tackle. Mr. Scheible ran a stagecoach that picked up passengers at the various hotels and boardinghouses and transported them to the beach.

Summer guests at Scheible's boardinghouse pose for a picture. The formal attire of the guests was not just for the photo—it was typical for the day.

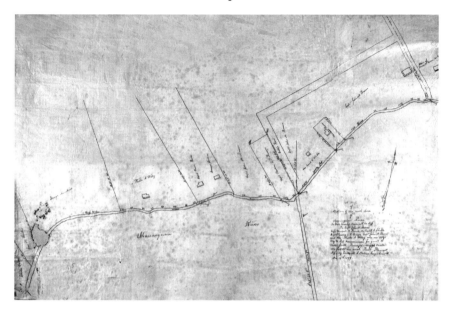

This survey map, prepared in 1879, shows Brielle property line divisions on the Manasquan River in the vicinity of today's Brown Street.

After Captain James Henry Green died in 1878, Catherine Louisa Green Smart, one of Captain Henry's daughters, remodeled the Green homestead into a hotel and called it Smart's Hotel. Later, it was known as "Ocean View House," and Mr. William Reed was the proprietor. This building is still standing at 620 Green Avenue, next to the present Union Landing Restaurant.

THE BRIELLE LAND ASSOCIATION

The process by which Union Landing became known as Brielle is an interesting one. In the late 1800s, Union Landing, as Brielle was known in those days, was still a part of Wall Township and consisted mainly of farms. The rise of railroads had diminished the importance of the coasting trade, the seagoing transportation mode for which Union Landing was a center. There was no industry to speak of, and roads were primitive at best. Union Landing was a remote location on a riverbank connecting to the open ocean—the ideal place to build a seaside retreat. Development began in earnest when Mr. Mellon of the Union League Club of Jersey City vacationed in Squan Village and told the other club members about it. Some of them had also visited the Jersey Shore. They all decided to look into purchasing some property for development in the Squan Village vicinity. Mr. Mellon knew of the Hank Voorhees farm, which he believed could be purchased at a reasonable price. They gave the name Brielle to their seaside resort because Mr. Mellon had recently visited a town in Holland named Brielle. The windmills and the harbor in the area they were considering reminded him of that town. A committee was set up to look at the property.

In 1881, Mr. Mellon, together with Messrs. Turner, Bacot and Behringer, three principals of the newly formed Brielle Land Association, purchased 150 acres of land east of the present Union Avenue. This property was bounded by Union Avenue, the Manasquan River estuary, the Glimmer Glass and the present Woodland Avenue. Three streets were laid out: Magnolia Avenue, Park Avenue (later renamed Fisk Avenue) and Woodland Avenue. The property was surveyed and laid out in lots of 50 by 150 feet. These lots sold for $250. There were smaller lots along Woodland Avenue (50 by 100 feet), which sold for $150. They also purchased 12 acres of land from Samuel Hanaway in the area of the present Crescent Drive, off Green Avenue. Presumably as a part of their plan, the tract was bisected by a branch of the recently constructed New York and Long Branch Railroad.

The developers wisely donated a parcel of land to the railroad company for the purpose of building a railroad station. The members of the Brielle Land Association wanted to have a train station with regular train service to the area. A regular station stop on this line enabled easy access to and from New York, Philadelphia and all points in between. In those days, one could travel south and then west on the railroad all the way to Philadelphia. With this in mind, they wined and dined Mr. Blodgett, superintendent of the New York and Long Branch Railroad, who promised them a station. It was built in 1881 and stood by the tracks between Woodland and Park Avenues. The train would make scheduled stops at the station or on signal or to let passengers off. Even freight trains would drop off freight that was marked "Put off at Brielle Station." Since the station was called Brielle, more people started calling the area Brielle, and with the decrease in the coasting trade, the name Union Landing began to fade away.

At the time the Brielle Land Association was selling vacation cottages, the already prosperous hotel trade flourished like never before. This was no doubt greatly facilitated by the new Brielle railroad station. There were still very few permanent residents of the area, but the population swelled in the summer months with well-to-do families from the cities. They would spend the entire summer season in Union Landing, either at a hotel or in

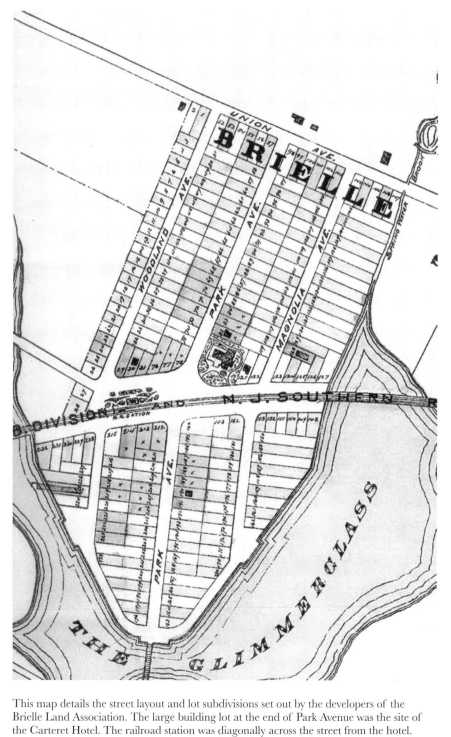

This map details the street layout and lot subdivisions set out by the developers of the Brielle Land Association. The large building lot at the end of Park Avenue was the site of the Carteret Hotel. The railroad station was diagonally across the street from the hotel.

COTTAGE OF J. R. TURNER.

This was a typical vacation cottage built by the Brielle Land Association. Most of the original Stick-style cottages have been demolished to make way for new construction, but a few still remain.

M. K. KELLAM, Pres.,   H. D. BACOT, Sec.,   NELSON J. H. EDGE, Treas.,
74 Murray Street, N. Y.   Jersey City.   Merchants' Bank, Wall St., N.Y.

BRIELLE.

This new summer resort is situated in the Township of Wall, Monmouth County, N. J., midway between New York and Philadelphia, with which cities, as well as the principal towns of New Jersey, it has direct daily communication by the unequalled facilities of the New Jersey Central and Pennsylvania Railroads, and their branches; both of these trunk roads using the route in common.

A handsome and conveniently arranged Railroad Station, with lawn, evergreens and flowers, is in the centre of the property.

The Avenues are wide, well graded and gravelled, bordered with shade trees. The Cottage Plots are large, covered with grassy soil, and many have desirable water frontages.

The well known facilities for Bathing, Boating, Sailing, Fishing and Gunning afforded by the Manasquan River and its Inlet to the Ocean are unequalled by any other resort on the entire New Jersey coast.

A spacious family Hotel is in progress of erection on the property, to be finished and ready for the reception of guests on the 1st of May, 1883. Several handsome Cottages lately finished in the Queen Anne style and in the immediate vicinity of the Hotel, are for sale at moderate prices and on easy terms. Families owning, renting or erecting Cottages on the lands of the Association will be able to procure their meals at this Hotel, and thereby avoid this inconvenience of housekeeping during the summer vacation.

A good supply of spring water will be conveyed through the Avenues from Water Works to be erected on the property.

For Maps and Prices of Building Plots, Cottages, &c., and any further information in regard to the property, apply to

This print advertisement was published by the Brielle Land Association to promote its new vacation venture at the shore.

This is the Brielle train station shown from the street side of the building. This photo may have been taken from the Hotel Carteret across the street. Note the primitive conditions of the roads that were typical at the time.

rental cottages or in their own summer homes. Activities enjoyed by these early tourists included swimming, sailing and picnicking on nearby Osborn Island, also known as Treasure Island. Robert Louis Stevenson christened it that while vacationing here because it reminded him of the fictional island he created for his novel *Treasure Island*. The book had been published seven years earlier and Stevenson was well known because of it. Contrary to local legend, the island did not serve as his inspiration for the novel.

Fishing had not yet gained the popularity it would enjoy here in the future. In later years, Union Landing became a center for the developing motorboat industry. Local sailboat turned motorboat builder S. Bartley Pearce was a pioneer in powerboat racing. In the early twentieth century, Pearce brought the prestigious Harmsworth Racing trophy home to America after winning the 1907 International Cup Race on Long Island Sound near Oyster Bay.

The Brielle Land Association built the Hotel Carteret about 1884. It was located on Park Avenue near the railroad tracks. Park Avenue was called the "Road to the Beach" since it extended eastward via a bridge across the Glimmer Glass and connected to the north end of Manasquan Beach. Dances were held in the hotel, and a bar was located in the basement. The Brielle Land Association also built a bowling alley and a boathouse and provided a ball field for the amusement of the guests. A bathhouse was erected on the ocean beach at the end of the Road to the Beach. The area of Manasquan Beach at the end of the present Brielle Road was known as "Brielle Beach." Charlie Longstreet ran a stage for the convenience of the guests for a fare of ten cents for the ride back and forth. The use of the bathhouse cost twenty-five cents.

The Hotel Carteret, or the Carteret Arms as it was sometimes called, was later sold to Mr. Jake Fields, a Wall Street broker, who renamed it the Brielle. A few years later, a chef named Switzer bought it and called it Hotel Switzer. It was later sold to Mr. Gerlach, who converted it into a military academy for boys named the Gerlach Academy.

THE GERLACH ACADEMY

In the last decade of the nineteenth century, a nationally recognized military school that catered to carriage trade patronage was established here in Brielle. The Brielle Land Association, incorporated in 1881, erected a fine new Queen Anne–style hotel at what is now the corner of Brielle Avenue and Fisk Avenue (in those days called Park Avenue). Following two or three owners, the building went up for sale and was purchased in 1895 by D. Gerlach, who established the Gerlach Academy. He and his family resided at the academy. Prior to establishing the school in Brielle, Gerlach had operated a military school in College Point, New York, also called Gerlach Academy. Housed in the former Boker Mansion, the school had operated there for a number of years before the building was converted into the College Point Club, a hotel. Perhaps Gerlach was attracted to Brielle for the same reasons as many of the wealthy summer visitors. According to the brochure:

> *The Gerlach Academy is incorporated under the laws of the State of New Jersey. The work of the pupils is at all times open to the inspection of the State Board of Education. The high character of the work performed by us as educators, and the excellent results obtained, have received the commendation and approval of the State Board of Regents.*

One of Mr. Gerlach's ads in *Scribner's* in April 1900 regarding this military boarding school states, "Prepares [boys] for American and European Universities. Located in one of the prettiest spots on the Jersey shore—truly an ideal spot for a boy's school." In larger print, the ad continues: "WE WILL TAKE CARE OF YOUR BOYS DURING YOUR VISIT TO PARIS." Another advertisement indicates:

Real Estate Development and the Rise of Tourism

Getting ready for the battle of life includes something more than mental equipment at Gerlach Academy. *It means the training of boyhood into noble manhood…surrounded with the most healthful condition.*

The academy's brochure boasts, "Brielle is one of the most healthy spots on the Jersey coast." It goes on to state:

The school has its own electric plant, which lights the buildings and grounds. [Further,] no instructor has at any time more than six pupils in his class [and] the younger pupils are at all times under supervision, which prevents the formation of bad habits…The charge for board, room and tuition is $500 per year of twelve months. This sum includes care of underclothing, books, stationery and laundry…The regular vacations are at Christmas and at Easter, when pupils are allowed to spend the holidays at home.

On Thanksgiving, parents were expected to take dinner with the headmaster, instructors and pupils at the school. Remember, this was a twelve-month school year. "Pupils must write at least once a week to their parents. They may write more frequently at their pleasure." Among the necessary personal items needed to be brought by the students were

four outing shirts, without collars, six pairs of stockings, six pairs of cuffs, six standing collars and one napkin ring…The School Uniform is of dark blue, with white stripes, and costs $14.00–$16.00. Uniform Cap, $2.50. The school tailor makes this cap. During the summer the khaki uniform is worn.

According to the "General Rules and Regulations":

Students must rise promptly at first bugle call (6:00 AM) and must fall in line in upper hall at second bugle (6:10 AM)…No talking is permitted when line is descending or ascending the stairs…Lounging about the grounds or building will result in the forfeiture of recreation period…No disobedience or insolence will be tolerated from any pupil.

Times for each activity of the day were laid out in the same way, and lights out was set at 9:00 p.m. "On Saturday and Sunday afternoons from 1 to 5:30, students are free to employ the time as they choose. They must not, however, visit at houses without the consent of the principal."

The building burned down sometime after 1908 and was not rebuilt.

The Hotel Carteret, as it fronted Park Avenue. If one continued on the road toward the right and crossed the train tracks, a bridge connected the Brielle development to Manasquan Beach.

NOTABLE GUESTS AT UNION LANDING

In addition to the well-known hotels and boardinghouses mentioned here, many people in the area who had spare rooms were willing to rent them to summer visitors. More and more people started coming to the area to vacation.

Probably the most famous visitor to Brielle was the author Robert Louis Stevenson. He was ill with tuberculosis and stayed at Saranac, New York, for a time, but he had grown tired of that locale. His artist friend Will H. Low suggested a visit to the Union House on the Manasquan River. Arriving in May 1888, before the busy season started, Stevenson spent about a month there resting, walking, sailing on the river in a hired catboat and, on rainy days, writing chapters of his novel *The Master of Ballantrae*. He wrote a note to fellow author Sidney Colvin describing his vacation spot:

> *We are here at a delightful country inn, like a country French place, the only people in the house, a catboat at our disposal, the sea always audible on the outer beach, the lagoon as smooth as glass, all the queer many colored villas standing shuttered and empty; in front of ours across the lagoon, two long wooden bridges, one for rail, one for the road, sounding intermittent traffic. It is a highly pleasant and delightful change from Saranac.*

Real Estate Development and the Rise of Tourism

Many stories have been told about Stevenson and the island in the Manasquan River, which has been called Osborn Island, Treasure Island, Osprey Island and now, officially, Nienstedt Island in honor of the family who donated it to the Borough of Brielle. Stevenson had published *Treasure Island* in 1883, years before coming to this area. His friend Will Low wrote the following account of one of his many river excursions with Stevenson in his *Chronicle of Friendship*:

> One afternoon we landed on an island a little way up the river, whose shore on one side was protected by a bulkhead. As the island was nameless, we proceeded to repair the oversight and christened it Treasure Island, after which we fell to with our pocket knives to carve the name upon the bulkhead, together with our initials and the date.

At the end of May 1888, Stevenson left this area to board a yacht that his wife had hired to sail to the South Seas. He died at his home in Samoa in 1894.

Other famous people who stayed at the Union House were sculptor Augustus Saint-Gaudens, publisher Charles Scribner, artist John Singer Sargent and the already mentioned illustrator and designer Will H. Low.

MANASQUAN RIVER ARTISTS

During the last two decades of the nineteenth century, a group of young American painters, many of whom had recently returned from periods of study in Europe, began to arrive in Brielle, New Jersey. The artist Will Hicok Low first appears in 1884 in the *Manasquan Seaside*, under the column "Union Notes," as among those registered at the Union House. He is described as being from Brooklyn and visiting with his family. In 1872, Low had made his debut as an exhibitor at the National Academy of Design. It was at this exhibition that Low first met fellow artist Wyatt Eaton, who was to become Low's greatest and closest friend. In 1885, Low was asked by a publisher to choose a book of poems of his choice to illustrate. Low decided on a work by Keats titled *Lamia*. At once, he came to Brielle to work on the task, using local folks as models for his illustrations. When *Lamia* was published, it became an immediate success, selling over two thousand copies in an expensive edition costing fifteen dollars. In 1889, Low was honored by the World's Fair in Paris when he received a medal for his *Lamia* illustrations.

Low greatly enjoyed the area around the Manasquan River and brought many artist friends, including Robert Louis Stevenson, to visit over the next decade. Even Thomas Eakins could be seen at the local beaches during the 1880s. Both Eakins and Low worked as faculty at the school of the National Academy of Design in New York—Eakins employed as a lecturer and Low working as an instructor in painting.

Low's friend Wyatt Eaton, one of the founding members of the highly important American Artists Association, was present in 1888 when a farewell party for Robert Louis Stevenson was held at the farm of Nestor and Caroline V. (Carrie) Sanborn in neighboring Point Pleasant Beach. Eaton, Stevenson and the sculptor Augustus Saint-Gaudens had all been friends of Low during their student days in France. Low arranged for his friend Saint-Gaudens to finish his famous bas-relief portrait of Stevenson while Stevenson was vacationing in Brielle. Carrie Sanborn was a close friend of Low and Eaton. During the summer months, Carrie taught classes in landscape painting in and around Brielle. She would often have her students, many of whom were members of the Brooklyn Artists, stay at the Union House. In early September 1894, Theodore Robinson, one of the first and greatest of America's impressionist painters, took over Sanborn's classes as guest instructor. During his stay in Brielle, Robinson painted what are considered two of his best paintings: *Draw Bridge, Longbranch Rail Road* (collection of the National Gallery, Washington, D.C.) and *The Landing.* In 2003, *The Landing* was sold at auction in New York, where it fetched the price of $2,100,000.

In the late 1890s, two new artists, Albert G. Reinhart and Charles Freeman, took up permanent residence in Brielle. During the late 1870s, both were students of Frank Duveneck, an American teacher working near Munich, Germany. Duveneck originally came to the area to study at the Munich Academy, as did his friend William Merritt Chase. However, when the next group of Americans came to Munich, some preferred the teaching methods of Duveneck, who had recently begun taking on students. The best of these students were labeled "the Duveneck Boys." They included John Twachtman, John White Alexander (who was later to become the president of the National Academy), Albert Reinhart and Charles Freeman. After completing their European art training, both Freeman and his close friend Reinhart began visiting the Jersey Shore, looking for a suitable place to settle. By 1900, both had taken up residence in Brielle, where they remained for the rest of their lives.

Real Estate Development and the Rise of Tourism

This is an original oil painting by impressionist Charles Freeman. The painting shows Freeman's house on Green Avenue looking toward the river. This is the view Freeman would have seen looking east through the windows of his studio.

These Brielle painters were artists who had received the best educations available to young American painters. It is our great opportunity to acknowledge their lives and accomplishments as members of the historical Brielle art community.

About 1910, in order to supplement their income, Catherine Freeman, the wife of impressionist painter Charles H. Freeman, opened the Three Cedars Tea House at their riverfront home at 504 Green Avenue. Afternoon tea and desserts were served on the lawn facing the river in nice weather or on the glassed-in porch on rainy or cool days. Mr. Freeman's studio was on the property by the street. Both buildings still stand.

The place became very popular, and many famous people visited there, including silent screen actress Mary Pickford. In later years, Fred Astaire and his sister Adele, writer Albert Payson Terhune and radio commentator Lowell Thomas also visited there.

The Freemans' house as it appeared when it was the Three Cedars Tea House. Charles Freeman used the garage building to the right as his studio.

Mrs. Reinhart opened an art gallery where her husband's works were sold.

The year 1899 marked the formation of the Manasquan River Yacht Club. Frederick J. Folk founded it for the purpose of gathering together the yachting enthusiasts in the area to form a racing club. In 1900, the first commodore, Willard S. Fisk, and other officers and trustees were selected. The first clubhouse was a rented ice cream pavilion owned by Theodore S.P. Brown. In 1905, the club purchased the Wylie estate, which is its present site. The club's activities added to the interest in sailboat racing, and many social events, such as dances, were held there for the members.

When the automobile arrived in the early 1900s, it brought more vacationers and greatly increased the mobility of visitors and residents alike. Hotels and other businesses flourished here. A postcard sent from Captain Brown's hotel in the early 1900s recounts the following:

Dear M,

This house is kept by Captain Brown's daughter (Mrs. Wainwright). Do you remember the place? We knew it as Manasquan—the name & P.O. address are changed to Brielle—We have enjoyed our trip, sailing, crabbing, watching the bathers at the beach and bringing to mind the old times as much as possible—the town is much improved—we find very elegant cottages here—new and good state roads. Automobiles numerous stages to the beach & carriage driving pleasant—have been to Point Pleasant, Barnegat, Sea Girt, etc. How much I wonder can you recall—wish you and Mr. R were here too.

Love from
Mrs. W.L.S.

BART PEARCE: MASTER BOAT BUILDER

One of the well-known spots on the riverfront in Brielle was Pearce's Boatyard, located where the Brielle Marine Basin is today. Shem Bartley Pearce (called Bart) was the son of Captain Shem Pearce, who was a master of deep-sea sailing vessels that rounded Cape Horn many times. Shem was also an excellent builder of local schooners, skiffs and sloops. Bart took his father's place and became one of the most prominent boat builders in Monmouth County. His boats were much in demand by members of the Manasquan River Yacht Club, of which he was a charter member.

In 1906, Bart became interested in motorboat racing. Mr. Edward Schroeder, a summer visitor from Jersey City, urged him to accept the command of the *Dixie*, built by Clinton Crane and purchased by Mr. Schroeder. It was entered in the Harmsworth Trophy Race to challenge the British contender on the English Channel. Established in 1903, the Harmsworth Trophy Race was the first International Powerboat Race and not only pitted wealthy boat owners against one another but was also considered a challenge between nations. It is generally considered the powerboating equivalent of the America's Cup. Bart agreed, and soon people lined the Manasquan River bank to watch the *Dixie* trial runs with Captain Pearce at the helm. Under sponsorship of the Motorboat Club of America, the *Dixie* won the race and brought the Harmsworth Trophy to America for the first time in 1907.

Captain S. Bartley Pearce onboard the *Dixie II* with his crew. This photograph was taken along the Hudson River in New York, where many of the *Dixie*'s early test runs were conducted.

In 1908, the *Dixie II* was built for Mr. Schroeder by C.F. Wood of City Island, New York. Bart Pearce captained this boat also and won the Harmsworth Trophy a second time.

Pearce's Boatyard continued to flourish, and Bart Pearce built many motor yachts and rowing bateaux after his retirement from racing.

When Mr. Schroeder died, he was interred in a large mausoleum in Greenwood Cemetery. The cemetery had been established in 1899 on what was once Captain John Brown's cow pasture.

THE MORGANS

In 1872, Jasper Morgan was born in Rice, Virginia. Jasper was the youngest of thirteen children born to former slaves Indiana and Robert Morgan. When he was about fifteen years old, Jasper signed on as a merchant seaman aboard a schooner bound for Boston. Jasper eagerly embarked on this new adventure but, never having travelled by boat before, was unprepared for the rigors of a sailor's life. Rough seas and seasickness did not agree with Jasper. After making port in Boston, Jasper left the sailor's life behind for good. He returned to his native Virginia by any and all land transportation available, including walking. About 1893, Jasper Morgan again left his home in Virginia, bound for nearby Manasquan, New Jersey. Jasper became a coach driver in Manasquan for Mr. Van Note, who owned a funeral parlor there. Soon after, Jasper began working for the Harty Poland Company as a house mover. In those days, houses were smaller and lighter than they are today and had no utility connections. Furthermore, the beach house lots in Manasquan were leased to the occupants. They owned the structure but not the land. If a homeowner bought a plot of land elsewhere, it was simply easier to move the house than to construct a new dwelling on the lot. In those early pre-automobile days, houses were moved on wheels pulled by teams of horses.

In 1900, Jasper married the former Mattie Harvey of Plainfield, New Jersey. Their five children, Edward, William, Mable, Jasper and Magnolia, began the extensive Morgan family tree. Many of their descendants still live in the area today. Soon after they married, Jasper and Mattie moved to a house on South Street in Brielle, near the western end of Borrie Avenue. Within a few years of moving there, Jasper was able to purchase the house and so became the first black landowner in Brielle. Homeownership was an impressive achievement for the son of former slaves, but it was not an individual accomplishment. Jasper and Mattie were part of the core of a close-knit community of blacks that began to develop in this area. Barter and trade of goods and services were the norm—a mason would help construct a new house for a hog farmer in exchange for meat. Despite this close sense of community among themselves, not all locals accepted their new black neighbors. New Jersey has had a long history of Ku Klux Klan activism, and Brielle was not exempt. One night in the early 1900s, a crowd of white-sheeted men erected and burned a cross on the Morgans' front lawn. Undeterred by these actions, Jasper came outside with his shotgun to face the Klansmen. Brielle at the time was an even smaller town than it is now, so despite their masks, the identities of Morgan's antagonists were not quite so secret. Morgan admonished them each by name and told them to go home.

In 1905, Jasper started his own business, becoming Brielle's first black business owner. He began clearing sand from the Manasquan and Brielle Beaches and transporting it by horse and wagon to locations where it was needed for construction, fill or road maintenance. His business prospered, and he hired many young black men in the area to work for him and also brought friends and family members from his home state of Virginia to the Brielle area to work with him. To this day, most of the Morgan, Harvey, Laws, Kenney and Moon families can trace their ancestry back to the same area in Prince Edward County, Virginia. Jasper's hauling company also collected trash from Brielle residents and was responsible for grading many streets laid out in Manasquan, Sea Girt, Wall Township and in his own Brielle neighborhood: Harris, Borrie and Bradley Avenues, as well as the cross street known then as Pleasant Parkway. Years later, Pleasant Parkway was renamed Morgan Parkway in honor of Jasper.

Not only an industrious worker and family man, Jasper was also a religious man. Together with his wife Mattie, he held prayer meetings in their home

Jasper Morgan is pictured here about 1920 behind one of his teams of horses. As Brielle's first black business owner, Morgan ran a successful fill and hauling business.

for friends and family. Not satisfied without a place to worship, he purchased the plot of land where the Shiloh Baptist Church stands today. It is said that Jasper got a bit of a raw deal on the property since at the time it was subject to significant flooding. The lot bordered Judah Creek in Manasquan. At the time, Judah Creek was still a substantial waterway that flowed through what is today Abe Voorhees Plaza in downtown Manasquan. Undeterred by the problem, Jasper simply hauled fill to the site to abate the flooding problem. From humble beginnings in a borrowed tent erected on the site, Shiloh Baptist Church was founded in 1909; the present church building was constructed in 1913. The congregation that grew from Jasper and Mattie's prayer meetings continues to flourish today on the eve of its 100th anniversary.

THE BRIELLE POST OFFICE

Bart Pearce was a fine carpenter. He built several houses in the area, as well as the Green Avenue post office, which opened in 1914. The building still stands today. Mr. Henry Kroh was the postmaster, assisted by his daughter Ananette. Interestingly, this public building was built without any bathroom facilities. Being in proximity to the Krohs' residence, it didn't create a major problem, but the post office would have to close periodically during the day while Henry or Ananette ran home. This post office, like many in small towns in the early 1900s, also sold general merchandise to the residents. As reported by Patricia Kroh Hendricks in her article "The Post Office on Green Avenue" in the Union Landing Historical Society's book *Union Landing Revisited*, the method of delivery of the mail to and from Brielle was very interesting:

> *Twice daily postal deliveries were bagged and thrown at the Green Avenue railroad crossing from two trains heading south from New York City. The bags were then loaded on a wheelbarrow to be pushed past Dr. Macy's cornfield, now a borough park, to the post office a block away. This chore was done either by the postmaster or assistant regardless of weather. Outgoing mail was picked up by a U.S. Mail employee riding in the baggage car of a train heading north from Bay Head Junction. The bagged mail was placed on a white platform close to the northbound track and fastened with string to what can only be described as a "hangman" structure. The locked grey bag dangled, waiting to be snatched by a long pole with a hook on the end as the train reduced speed and the baggage man leaned far out with the pole in hand.*

Real Estate Development and the Rise of Tourism

Miss Ananette Kroh became postmaster after her father's death in 1927. She told a very interesting story about train service at the Brielle railroad station:

> *During the summer months of 1915–1917, if you were going to Spring Lake, Asbury Park, New York, or points between, you would buy your ticket from the ticket agent at the Brielle station. When the train left Point Pleasant, the agent would place a large green and white flag in the socket between the tracks as a signal to the engineer to stop his train and take on one or more passengers. The ticket agent closed his window early and went home, so it was necessary for the would-be traveler, after dinner, to plant the flag himself and see that it was placed inside the station before the train stopped. The after dark traveler had a real problem. He had to take with him a tightly rolled newspaper and matches—lots of matches if the night was stormy. At the station when he judged the train had reached the bridge over the Manasquan River, he would light one end of the paper and wave it up and down or from side to side, praying meanwhile that the engineer would see it. Happy was the traveler when the signal was acknowledged with a cheery toot-toot of the engine's whistle. There was then time to trample the burning paper until no spark remained before the train stopped.*

THE GREAT WAR

For information on how World War I affected this area, the memoirs of Helen Leavens Winters are a good eyewitness source. Her family spent their summers in a house they had built in the winter of 1913–14. The house is still standing at 512 Green Avenue:

> *The outbreak of World War I in Europe during the summer of 1914 touched our lives in relatively minor ways. Food costs rose; sugar went from five to fifteen cents a pound in a week's time. Drug prices rose 100%. Housewives were urged to fight profiteers, and the Manasquan Fish Pound Company was accused of hoarding fish for higher prices. But Sarajevo was an ocean and half a continent away; we in the United States felt insular and protected. The man in small towns such as Brielle was inclined to keep himself aloof from the fracas those hot-headed Europeans had started.*
>
> *When we went to Brielle in the summer of 1917, it was a different story. Fresh from writing speeches to promote Liberty Loan Bond drives at school, we were surprised to see our railroad bridge patrolled by soldiers and to hear of local boys who had been drafted into the army. President*

Wilson was now saddled with the awesome responsibility of guiding his country at war.

War industries were crying for help, and girls who had been in domestic service were being lured into factories by higher wages and shorter hours. Mother was hard pressed to find and keep any kind of household help.

The war was brought rather forcefully to the Jersey Shore by the news that a German U-boat had shelled Fort Hancock on Sandy Hook. The fact of danger right off the beaches must have been sobering to local residents. The government tried to keep the event a secret, but to no avail.

The following is a list of Brielle men who served in World War I:

Bailey, Fred F.

Clayton, Cecil S.

Dexter, Alan P.

Donnelly, Arthur G.

Johnston, Raymond F.

Jonscher, Paul H.

Langworth, Cort. V.

Lloyd, Edward

Marcellus, Hendrick V.

McCarty, Floyd C.

Schwemler, Robert J.

VanSickel, George

Voorhees, Abram D.

Although not technically Brielle residents, three other young men merit mentioning—Clinton E. Fisk, William A. Higgins and John Langdon Norris. They were only part-time residents of Brielle, but these young men were among the tens of thousands of Americans who made the supreme sacrifice for their country. Captain Clinton E. Fisk was the only son of Colonel Willard C. Fisk, commander of the 107th United States Infantry. The senior Fisk had been sent home on medical leave during the summer of 1918. His son was acting as a major in command of the 1st Battalion of the 107th in Flanders when he was killed in action on October 18, 1918. The Fisks were summer residents of Brielle. William Higgins's family were natives of Brooklyn, New York. He left behind his parents, three brothers and two sisters. His father was in the importing business, and they also summered in Brielle. Norris was married to Brielle resident Elizabeth Faison. Their son was born in March of the following year.

After the Armistice was declared on November 11, 1918, things gradually returned to normal. Union Landing by that time had definitely become known as Brielle.

CHAPTER 6

BRIELLE, NEW JERSEY, INCORPORATED 1919

FORMATION OF THE BOROUGH OF BRIELLE

On April 10, 1919, the New Jersey state legislature passed an act establishing Brielle as an independent borough, pending approval by registered voters within the boundaries of the proposed municipality. The question was put on the ballot at a special election held on May 6, 1919. At the time of the election, Brielle was a tiny portion of Wall Township, which extended from Brielle in the south to the Shark River to the north and inland for some five miles. Local leaders observed that Brielle's tax base contributed nearly one-third of Wall Township's tax revenue, and the area received comparatively little in return. When the act was debated in the legislature, various attempts were made to defeat it. Opponents of the measure contended that the act was "partisan" or "politically motivated." Their arguments did not hold up in the legislature, as the bill gained support from both Republicans and Democrats in Trenton. In fact, the bill was initially sponsored by state senator Henry E. Ackerson, a Democrat, and had support in the assembly from T. Lloyd Lewis, a Republican. Petitions showing support of nearly half of the registered voters of the proposed municipality confirmed the public's support for the act. Many opponents of the measure readily admitted that their opposition was based mainly on the fear that the new borough would, upon separation from Wall Township, then be responsible for providing its own municipal services, thus putting strain on the new isolated tax base. Proponents of the act countered that the monies currently being raised for Wall's tax coffers would be better and more efficiently spent locally in the new borough. Those promoting the separation also pointed out that there were no immediate plans to make municipal improvements that would put a strain on the tax base. The Wall Township Board of Education had, in fact, just constructed a brand-new school building at the corner of Union Avenue and Union Lane, which is Brielle Borough Hall today. Furthermore, it was widely believed that officials chosen from the local population would be better able to govern Brielle with the wishes and views of the local residents in mind.

When the ballots were counted, the referendum passed by a wide margin. Out of ninety-nine votes cast, sixty-six were in favor of secession and thirty-one against. Two ballots were rejected as invalid. Once established as a borough, the wheels were set in motion to elect the officials to govern and operate the new "Baby Borough" of the Jersey coast. Another special election was scheduled for June 3, 1919, to elect a mayor, six councilmen, a tax assessor, a tax collector and a justice of the peace. The deadline for filing petitions to run for office was May 29, 1919. Richard Donnelly was the sole candidate for mayor and both parties endorsed him. The candidates for councilman included John S. Rankin, Wilbur Allen, John Bennett, Fred Newman, John H. Folk, James Brewer, Theodore J.R. Brown and Edward L. Edwards. Candidates for tax assessor were Harry Van Ness and Robert Rankin, and the candidates for tax collector were Ralph Pearce and Edward Stires. No petitions were filed for the office of justice of the peace. On June 3, seventy-one voters went out to the polls and elected Richard Donnelly the first mayor of Brielle. Along with Donnelly, three Republicans and three Democrats were elected to the borough council. John H. Folk, Edward L. Edwards and Theodore J.R. Brown were the Republican victors for council seats, while James Brewer, Wilbur Allen and John W. Bennett were the Democrats elected to office.

On June 9, 1919, the newly incorporated borough of Brielle held its first council meeting in the upstairs room of the Brielle Fire Company headquarters. An article in the *Asbury Park Evening Press* on June 7, 1919, stated:

> *Brielle is to start life anew tomorrow night with the organization of its first mayor and council. The men selected as the first officers of the baby borough of the North Jersey Coast at the elections last Tuesday have already been sworn in and everything is in readiness for the municipality to launch forth under its new form of government.*

Early council minutes relate in great detail the settling of financial accounts with Wall Township and the establishment of basic municipal services for the residents of Brielle, including creating committees to address the needs of the community. The original committees were finance, lights, streets, law and ordinance, printing, poor and fire. The newspaper went on to say:

Although it is the infant borough of the coast, Brielle is one of the largest. There is approximately three miles of riverfront and included in the territory is a high range of hills upon which many magnificent homes have been erected. Recently a new public school was erected in a central location. Its streets are excellent and the health conditions splendid. There are a total of 125 voters and this number will be greatly increased by many who have expressed their intention of becoming permanent residents here since the change in government.

Brielle's first mayor, Richard A. Donnelly, who served until 1922, was a successful businessman in Trenton. The first councilmen came from various walks of life and occupations. James Brewer was superintendent of a large river shore estate. Another elected official, Wilbur Allen, was a painting contractor. John H. Folk was a retired businessman in the wholesale leather business. Theodore J.R. Brown, lawyer, was in the realty department of the Central Railroad of New Jersey. Edmund L. Edwards was a farmer. John Bennett's occupation was unknown, but he was regarded as one of the new borough's most well-known citizens. Robert L. Rankin, a contractor and builder, was elected tax assessor. Ralph T. Pearce, an expert mechanic, was chosen as tax collector.

The third public school in the area as it appeared when it was first built in 1918 at the corner of Union Avenue and Union Lane. Note that the right rear section of the building was not completed initially, but the roof formed an overhang supported by a column. That portion of the building was completed several years later, when more classroom space was required.

In 1919, the borough hall was on the second floor of the building that also served as the firehouse. That original building still stands at the site as part of today's firehouse. Among the first acts of the new governing body was the renaming of Bridge Avenue on August 18, 1919, to Higgins Avenue to honor William A. Higgins, a fallen soldier in World War I. The minutes actually report that Brielle Avenue, from Park Avenue to Union Lane, was designated as Higgins Avenue, but the earliest tax maps from 1919 do not support this. They clearly show Bridge Avenue renamed Higgins Avenue. In those days, the street was barely two blocks long, since State Route 35 did not yet exist. Higgins Avenue extended northward from the bridge, and one had to make a right turn at Union Avenue at the location of the present-day Constitution Park. The governing body also renamed Park Avenue, from Union Avenue to the Glimmer Glass, Fisk Avenue. This was done to honor Captain Clinton E. Fisk, who was killed near the end of World War I. The following letter from Fisk's father appears in the Minutes of the Council Meeting of September 15, 1919:

Honorable Richard Donnelly, Mayor

My Dear Mr. Mayor,
I have learned that the Council of the Borough of Brielle have taken official action changing the name of Park Avenue in the Borough to Fisk Avenue to honor the memory of my son, the late Captain Clinton E. Fisk who was killed in action in France, October 18th, 1918.

I desire through you to express to the members of the Council the appreciation of his family for this mark of respect. From early boyhood Captain Fisk spent his summers at Brielle and his associations and activities there were among the most intimate and enjoyable of his life.

He played a man's part in the greatest world drama of all time, and I express the hope that his sacrifice thus recognized and perpetuated by the action of the council may be an example for those who come after to follow.

Yours sincerely,
Willard C. Fisk

PROGRESS IN BRIELLE

Despite concerns by detractors over the cost of providing their own municipal services, the fledgling government was almost immediately put to work authorizing basic municipal improvements. Of primary concern was the condition of the streets. Most of the streets were dirt or gravel roads, and poor drainage was a common problem. Curbs needed to be constructed and paving needed to be maintained. Public utilities at that time were few and far between in this rural setting, but progress was coming. Two competing electric companies vied for the contract to provide electric streetlights and service to the new community. The northern company, the Atlantic Coast Electric Light Co., was headquartered in Asbury Park and the competing southern company, the Lakewood & Coast Electric Co., in Lakewood. As a result, Brielle was on the fringe of either service area. The borough in the end retained service from the Lakewood & Coast Electric Co., but the net result was at times poor service, particularly in the aftermath of a storm. Regular maintenance was an issue too—the early council frequently heard complaints regarding streetlight outages around town. This time period also saw the beginnings of pipeline gas service in the area.

Initially, Brielle's businesses and residents were supplied with drinking water from private wells. Geographically, Brielle sits in proximity to two major aquifers, the Englishtown Aquifer and the Kirkwood Aquifer. As a result, wells were relatively easy to drill. As the population density increased, the governing body made the decision to centralize the supply of water, no doubt having in mind the creation of a revenue stream. In 1927, a water department was formed, and initially the supply was furnished from the already established Manasquan Water Works. Water mains were laid, and the system expanded through a series of bond issues over the ensuing years. By 1929, the present water tower in the public works yard had been constructed and Brielle had its own independent water supply. Brielle's Water Department remained independent in this manner until the late 1980s, when increasing population and demand for water supply required the borough to form an alliance with four other towns—Wall Township, Spring Lake Heights, Sea Girt and Spring Lake—and create the Manasquan Reservoir Water Authority. This authority created the Manasquan River Reservoir and Water Treatment Plant that supplies a large portion of the subscribing townships' potable water.

BRIELLE'S BRAVEST AND BRIELLE'S FINEST

The Brielle Fire Department, originally known as Brielle Chemical Company No. 1, was organized on June 13, 1910, prior to the separation from Wall Township. At that time, this area was part of Wall Township Fire District

An early photograph of the members of the Brielle Fire Company from 1931. The man in the rear ringing the fire gong is George Legg, Brielle's first paid police chief.

No. 2. The first organizational meetings were held at Wainwright's General Store that was located in a building on Union Lane, next to the Union House. There were eleven charter members. The first chief was S. Bartley Pearce and the first president was Albert Ellis. Dues were ten cents per month. Fines for nonattendance at meetings were ten cents; for not answering a roll call at a false alarm, fifteen cents; and for not answering a roll call after a fire, twenty-five cents. The first firehouse was erected in 1910 on a lot purchased for $200 from John Bennett on Longstreet Avenue. The first fire engine was a horse-drawn/hand-drawn chemical wagon with two forty-five-gallon chemical tanks. Financial support initially came from dues, fines and support from firemen's wives, who held bazaars and similar activities.

There was no police department to speak of at our founding as a borough. Protection was provided as needed by various constables, special officers and sheriff's department officers. Upon incorporation, one of the first acts of the borough council was to appoint J. Wellington Pearce as marshal. He received no pay; however, they did make a concession to pay for his badge. In August

1919, Frank Pettit was named assistant marshal and went on to become marshal upon the retirement of Pearce from that unpaid job. Starting in 1923, the sole police officer would henceforth be referred to as chief of police. Shem Pearce was the first man appointed to that job by the mayor. Still an unpaid position, Pearce served in that capacity for two years and was succeeded by George Legg. Legg served the borough for many years, until his retirement in 1964. The mayor and council officially established a police department in 1933. At that point, Chief Legg became the first paid law enforcement officer in Brielle. Soon after, in 1934, John Rogers became the second police officer hired in Brielle.

THE BRIELLE PUBLIC LIBRARY

As happens rather frequently in Brielle, private citizens seeing a need step forward to address that need. The genesis of the current free public library is due to the work and generosity of one woman, Mrs. Mary W. Strong. She established a library in her home on Longstreet Avenue in September 1922 with fifty books, a complete file of *Century* magazines and high hopes.

Located on Longstreet Avenue, Applewood was the home of Mrs. Mary Strong and the location of the first public library in Brielle.

Mrs. Strong was a resident of Brielle for only two years when she began her venture. She had no formal training as a librarian but had started the first library in Suffern, New York, and then worked one year at the library in Point Pleasant. When an opportunity came to organize a system in Brielle, she seized it.

Miss Eleanor Randall was establishing the Monmouth County Library at this time. She broadcast an appeal for assistance, which Mary Strong answered. Together they planned to open the new venture in Brielle under the patronage of the parent-teacher association, of which Mrs. Strong was president. They planned to place their books in the local grammar school. Miss Randall objected to this. She felt that while the children could be reached, no contact would be made with the adults of the community.

She came to the Strong home for some discussions and immediately fell in love with the large old house, known as Applewood, built circa 1850. She suggested that this would be the ideal location for a library. She persuaded Mrs. Strong to agree with her. In September 1922, the Brielle library opened its doors to the public. Located in the sun parlor of the Strong home, it met with immediate and hearty approval.

Mrs. Strong, a mother of five young girls, was not only librarian and publicity agent for the new venture but janitor as well. Each Thursday before the door opened a fire had to be lit, shelves dusted, new books arranged and files set out.

The walls were solidly covered from the floor to half their height with books. A large table in the center of the room was used to display recent acquisitions and also as a checking desk. The table belonged to Mrs. Strong's father, Dr. Frank Williams of Trenton, who had used it as an operating table. A huge settee stood in the corner by the entrance, of which every inch was covered with books. At that time, if the small library did not have a book desired by a patron, Mrs. Strong could procure it from either Freehold or Newark by drawing on the county or state libraries. In those early days, the month of March saw the peak of circulation.

For the first eighteen years, Mrs. Strong not only supplied the home for the library but furnished the heat and light as well. She also paid for stationery, printed notices and materials for rebinding the books. In 1941, the borough finally came to her assistance by voting the library a yearly grant of $250.

The library remained in Mrs. Strong's house until 1949. The Brielle Board of Education had purchased property where the school is currently located that had been the Rankin farm, and the Rankin farmhouse was still there, about where the current school athletic field is located. The building remained idle until 1951, when pleas from town organizations to use it as a community center resulted in making two rooms available on the first floor for a public library to be open five and a half hours per week. Details were worked out with the school board, which had been using the building for kindergarten classes. Borough council appropriated $500 for bookshelves and necessary renovations to the rooms, and Mrs. Strong continued as librarian until 1954, when she resigned and moved away. Mrs. Myron (Betty) Taylor became the librarian on a voluntary basis until becoming a permanent librarian with professional status in March of that year. The Rankin house was used for only a short time, as it was soon sold and moved (to the Union Lane corner of Union Avenue) to make room for a new school.

In June 1954, the assembly hall in the basement of the old school, today the borough hall, became the town library. On March 16, 1955, the library committee signed articles of incorporation and the library became an independent organization. By November of that year, a constitution had been adopted and a board of trustees chosen. The first board president was Dr. Agnes R. Wayman. The budget that first year was $1,500. The library owned nine hundred books. Following Betty Taylor, Mrs. George (Ethel) Taylor served the library for fifteen years as director.

The Brielle Public Library, as an association library, received some funding from the borough. The association had been gathering funds for an eventual building project. In July 1986, the Brielle Council adopted a $380,000 bond ordinance to finance a new building. Then, in 1987, an ordinance was passed to increase the bond by $75,000 for a total of $455,000. The new facility was built on the site of the old Loughran Gardens wholesale retail showroom.

THE MANASQUAN RIVER GOLF CLUB

On September 8, 1922, the *Coast Star* commented:

> *A large group of citizens of wealth and enterprise, all either summertime or permanent residents of a big community of coast resorts on the Jersey shore just south of Asbury Park, last night added the lovely little Borough of Brielle, to the world of sports and country club life. The Manasquan River Golf and Country Club—destined, for many physical reasons, to be the best course on the coast—became an actuality at an enthusiastic meeting of the subscribing share-holders in the new-born club, the meeting being held in the splendid country home of Mr. Edwin Isham, River Road, Brielle, N.J.*

BRIELLE

The newspaper continues:

> *Brielle thus lands finally and definitely on the map, following the official announcement at the meeting that the club shares necessary to exercise the real estate option and secure forever the beautiful hills, rolling meadows, brooks and river frontage have now been subscribed for. The site selected is the only possible upland or hilly golf course along the New Jersey oceanfront.*

The cost to purchase the 140-acre Charles Osborn farm was $60,000, and it was noted that this amount was fully subscribed. It wasn't quite as smooth as that, however. A ninety-day, $1,000 option to purchase the property was within three days of expiration and was $10,000 short of the $60,000 goal. A meeting was held at the Isham home on September 23, and after much discussion, no additional money was pledged. About 10:30 p.m., the group decided to adjourn for some reason and then motor down to Bay Head to another member's house. In the car on the way, Howard Folk persuaded Edwin Isham to pledge the remaining $10,000 and stated that the club would deed him a small parcel of land next to his estate, which he had been attempting to purchase without success. In addition, the next $5,000 pledged would be the initial part of a payback. By the time they arrived in Bay Head, Isham agreed, and this was made known to the reassembled group. A purchase agreement was executed on September 26, 1922.

Along with Mr. Isham, one of the founding members of the golf and country club was his associate, Mr. Devoll. In their early years, both Mr. Isham and Mr. Devoll were singers. Mr. Isham was a baritone and Mr. Devoll a tenor. They both sang with several opera companies in the United States, in New York and Boston, and also with the Savoy Opera Company in England. Mr. Isham's family was in business in upstate New York, banking and importing tobacco. Mr. Devoll was married to Joanna Isham, Edwin Isham's cousin. Her family left the property that is now Isham Park in New York City.

After their singing careers ended, Mr. Isham and Mr. Devoll, in conjunction with other investors, built most of the "Studio" buildings on West Sixty-seventh Street in New York City. The building at 27 West Sixty-seventh was one of their first endeavors and is regarded as one of the most important multifamily buildings in the city. It is regarded as the beginning of successful apartment dwelling in the city as we know it today. Mr. Isham lived at 27 and Mr. and Mrs. Devoll lived across the street at 50 West Sixty-seventh. The Hotel des Artistes is another important building that these gentlemen were a part of. If you look at the Hotel des Artistes and the Musicians Building at 50 West Sixty-seventh, you can see a great similarity between the two buildings. They share a similar footprint and also their Gothic/Elizabethan architecture. They were also involved in the antique trade, dealing mainly in European furniture. As far as Isham and Devoll's house in Brielle is concerned, it seems that the two families may have shared the home. Mr. Isham died in 1933, and his obituary refers to the house as Lambert Hall. Mr. Devoll's obituary in 1937 refers to the house as Lamport Hall. It also speaks of the house being on Riverview Drive and claims that the funeral services for both men were held at the house. It is believed that the house referred to in both obituaries is the present estate at 836 Riverview Drive, which adjoins the golf club property on the riverfront.

Robert White of Wykagl was engaged to design an eighteen-hole course, with the first nine holes laid out on the southern portion of the property. Construction began quickly, and the cost for the first nine holes was about $3,000 per hole. These first new holes were played in June 1923. The other nine holes were located in the hilly and wooded upland section and were completed at a cost of about $5,000 per hole. To save money, all of the trees removed were cut into four-foot lengths and sold for firewood.

The first clubhouse was the Osborn farm homestead. That part of the building still stands and is the first section of the expanded facilities where the main entrance is now located. The first men's locker room was housed in a barn that was moved from Edwin Isham's property adjacent to the club property.

The first officers were John V.A. Cattus, 508 West End Avenue, New York, president; Edwin S. Isham, 27 West Sixty-seventh Street, New York, and summer home in Brielle, vice-president; T. Tasso Fischer, 429 Tremont Avenue, New York, treasurer; and Howard N. Folk of Brielle, secretary.

The club was viable financially until the onset of the Great Depression. On August 29, 1933, then president Bancroft Gheradi wrote to all members to call a special meeting because the club was in default on taxes and interest on the first mortgage. A plea had gone out to the members in the fall of 1932 asking any who could to subscribe to the needed cash amount of $4,000 to pay overdue indebtedness. The funds were not forthcoming. Efforts to raise the needed capital were unsuccessful, and some resulted in potential embarrassment to the club. An illegal slot machine was installed in the clubhouse in an attempt to raise capital. It worked for a while, but someone tipped off the Brielle Police. As Police Chief George Legg was seen approaching, the illicit machine was hastily removed via the back door, never to be brought back. The situation was dire and finally ameliorated by the third club president, Lee H. Bristol of Bristol Myers, who saved the club by writing personal checks to stay afloat. He was eventually repaid but had requested no interest on the amounts advanced. In 1935, the club was reorganized as the Manasquan River Golf Club.

After World War II, in 1946, the club again found itself in financial jeopardy and threatened with foreclosure on the mortgage. Mr. Bristol formed a syndicate with some other members, including local resident and big game fisherman Lou Marron, and raised enough money to refinance the mortgage. The land was thus saved from becoming a housing development.

In 1941, the club was looking to lure players and members to its links and noted the then current rates in the following advertisement:

Saturdays, Sundays and Holidays	*$2.00*
Other days	*$1.00*
Weekly	*$7.00*
Monthly	*$25.00*
Annual Dues (Including Tax)	*$50.00*

The ad further noted that visitors were welcomed. A post note advised that persons joining the club for a year would have included full privileges of the club and course for one of their children under twenty-one years of age.

When Brielle was first incorporated as a municipality, it was in practice little more than a farm town with a growing tourist industry. All that would change radically in the next decade. Several factors, including the establishment of national Prohibition, the reopening of the Manasquan Inlet and the beginnings of the fledgling sport fishing industry, came together to put Brielle on the map both literally and figuratively.

PROHIBITION AT THE JERSEY SHORE

In 1919, Congress passed the Eighteenth Amendment to the United States Constitution, making it illegal to purchase, sell, import or export alcoholic beverages within the United States. The amendment also gave Congress and the states the power to enforce this new law, while the related Volstead Act provided the definition of alcoholic beverages. Widely endorsed by the Women's Christian Temperance Union, the Anti-Saloon League and other conservative religious groups, the concept of national Prohibition probably had just as many, if not more, detractors, but they were not so well organized. The bill was ratified on January 16, 1919, and became effective one year later, on January 16, 1920. Once enacted, Prohibition was hailed by the temperance

This photograph shows the farmhouse on the Charles Osborn farm, with the children of the last tenant farmers on the porch, around the turn of the twentieth century. When the farm was sold in 1922, this house became the clubhouse of the Manasquan River Golf Club. The outline of this house can still be seen on the left side of the main building .

These are the barns and outbuildings behind the Charles Osborn homestead as they appeared in the early 1900s.

movement as social progress, but due to opposition in many states, notably New Jersey, it instead became a divisive force among the American people. In fact, Prohibition has often been referred to as America's second civil war in light of the violence and destruction that ensued as "wet" citizens literally went to war against "dry" citizens. Corruption in government and law enforcement was rife, and organized crime seized the opportunity to provide a product that was no longer commercially available. At the start of 1920, New Jersey was in a unique position to become a portal for illegal liquor to enter the country. Demand for the now illegal liquor was strong in the larger cities in New Jersey and New York, the coastal areas of New Jersey were still largely undeveloped and quick and easy access to unregulated international waters made New Jersey a mecca for liquor smuggling and rumrunning. The Manasquan River area was a prime conduit for the flow of illegal liquor into New Jersey.

Many early residents recall incidents when fast-moving motorboats would come into the Manasquan Inlet at night, being pursued by Coast Guard cutters. The men driving the motorboats were rumrunners, carrying their illicit cargo of liquor. The rumrunners began their journey three miles out in international waters, where freighters carrying liquor from Bermuda, the Caribbean Islands and Canada would congregate. That point outside U.S. jurisdiction became known as Rum Row. Liquor hidden in burlap sacks, wooden crates and even sealed inside tin cans was transferred to the rumrunners' fast motorboats,. The bootleggers would make the run to their customers onshore as fast as they could. Often, the same boat builders built the bootleggers' boats and the Coast Guard's boats. The builders could not admit to giving the bootleggers an unfair advantage over the United States government, but it was surely in their financial best interest to keep the booze flowing and make the Coast Guard boats just a little slower. In a ploy to escape the Coast Guard, the rumrunners would often head upriver through the railroad drawbridge, and the bridge tender would lower the span to block the Coast Guard pursuers. It seems that the bridge tenders were complicit with the smugglers as well. Occasionally, the bootleggers knew that they could not outrun the Coast Guard and were forced to jettison their cargo overboard. The bottles that washed ashore were eagerly harvested by local residents to stock their cellars.

MURDER IN BRIELLE

In the early 1930s, Brielle was still without an organized police department. That did not, however, imply a lack of need for one. Early council minutes relate instances of juvenile mischief, and there were also problems with vandalism at the Brielle train station. This was often a problem in the winter months, when the railroad company would close the station for the season. Years before he was employed as a paid police officer in the borough, John Rogers served under Chief George Legg as an unpaid special policeman.

On December 6, 1931, while serving in that capacity, Rogers and his friend Pete Moore were driving through the woods of the Wing estate. The estate consisted of a large house and several outbuildings on a plot of land that encompassed some forty-four acres. The property covered most of the area of the present-day Holly Hill Drive and Oceanview Road from Riverview Drive to what is today State Route 70. The northeast end of the property backed up to the Manasquan River Golf Club property. The only driveway in and out of the parcel extended through the woods to River Drive. The house was built in the early 1900s by Mr. Wing, a principal in the New York City–based Wing & Sons piano factory. Wing & Sons was a pioneer in the mass manufacturing of pianos. It became a leader in the business of mail-order pianos, which were usually shipped by rail to the train station closest to the customer's home. The factory was established in 1868 and remained active until about the 1930s. After the Wings sold the estate, it was operated for a time as a summer camp for boys by Jack Fish in the late 1930s and early 1940s. Fish subsequently operated a private school on the grounds called Brielle Academy. After the Fishes sold the property, it once again became a private residence. The home still stands today on Holly Hill Drive.

Rogers and Moore noticed an area where the dirt had been disturbed. Investigating closer, they stepped on a pile of leaves and saw blood ooze out. Nearby they saw glass bottles labeled "Muriatic Acid." Moore thought that someone had buried a deer, but Rogers disagreed. They left the area to get a shovel and, when they returned, began to dig. They uncovered the end of a shoe and then a foot inside the shoe. They went to get George Legg, who didn't believe the boys' story. By this time, it was late in the afternoon, and when Legg saw the body for himself he told Rogers to stand guard while he and Moore went to call the state police detectives.

By the time the troopers arrived it was dark, but they continued to work at exhuming the corpse. Once removed from the shallow grave, they could see that the man's facial features and fingerprints had been burned off with the acid. Rogers recalled that the chief removed a ring from the man's finger and part of the weakened flesh came off with it. They searched the body and found a watch and a driver's license loose in the man's pocket. The license identified him as James P. Granato of Keyport, New Jersey. Granato was alleged to be an enforcer for Chicago mob boss Al Capone. Because the

This dirt road on the Wing estate is near the site where James Granato's disfigured corpse was found in December 1931.

man's fingerprints and face had been burned off, a positive identification was never made. If the body was that of James Granato, he was probably in the area because of the illegal bootlegging activities. The following day, reporters and photographers from the *New York Daily News* arrived on the scene and photographed Rogers and Moore for the newspaper.

A DeSoto coupe registered to James Granato was recovered on a nearby farm in Wall Township. A hunter discovered it less than two miles from the site where the body was found. The car was brought to the state police station in Point Pleasant. The interior of the car was soaked with blood. The crime appears never to have been solved. The limited forensic tools available to the police at the time contributed to this, along with the condition of the body. DNA testing, facial reconstruction and other modern criminal investigative techniques would have gone a long way toward identifying the body had they existed. Add to that the history of corruption in Prohibition enforcement in New Jersey and it's easy to believe that there were those who would rather not have seen the crime investigated further.

This shallow grave is where Granato's body was hastily dumped and covered over before John Rogers and Pete Moore discovered it.

The interior of Granato's DeSoto coupe shows the aftermath of a violent Prohibition-era death.

A PERMANENT OPENING FOR THE MANASQUAN INLET

As mentioned previously, the depth and position of the Manasquan River Inlet varied greatly over the course of time. At times the inlet would become silted over and rendered impassable. Each of the four boroughs bordering the inlet—Manasquan, Point Pleasant, Point Pleasant Beach and now Brielle—would cooperate in financing the clearing of the mouth. The early council minutes record that on July 4, 1921, each of the four boroughs

Wooden dykes of this type were used to try to keep the Manasquan Inlet mouth open but were ineffective against the forces of nature.

appropriated $100 and appointed one representative to a committee led by S. Bartley Pearce to reopen the inlet. Within two weeks, the inlet was again opened, but the cost was double the amount that had been appropriated. In 1925, the construction of the Point Pleasant Canal connected the Manasquan River to the uppermost point of Barnegat Bay and a key section of the Intracoastal Waterway to Florida was completed. An unwanted side effect of the project was the complete closure of the Manasquan Inlet to the Atlantic Ocean. The river's natural outward flow into the ocean took the easier path through the canal and emptied into the bay. The inlet had periodically closed up over the centuries but never as completely as it did following the construction of the canal. Efforts by the four boroughs to maintain the opening were frequent and costly. This brought a virtual halt to maritime commerce, crippling the local economy.

A group known as the Manasquan River Protective Association had been formed to address the problems at the inlet. Upon the association's recommendation, each of the four boroughs was to appropriate $25,000 toward funding a project to be carried out by the U.S. Army Corps of Engineers to create a permanent inlet opening. The state and federal governments also contributed financially to the project. Brielle approved the measure on October 4, 1929, and the other municipalities followed suit. The Army Corps of Engineers began by constructing stone jetties outward into the ocean to define what would become the mouth of the inlet. The large stone boulders used in this phase of construction can still be seen today. The stones were brought to

After the inlet was permanently opened in 1931, the Coast Guard built a new station at Point Pleasant Beach. Note that the bulkheading on the Manasquan side of the inlet was not yet completed at the time of this photograph.

the area from an unusual source—construction on the New York City subway system. The stones were excavated during the construction of the Sixth Avenue IND subway line and transported by truck and rail to the inlet site. Once the jetties were complete, the work of removing the sand closing the mouth began. Steam shovels were used to excavate the sand, and the spoils were removed to a location farther upriver, now known as Sedge Island. The project was completed in July 1931. Once complete, the permanently reopened inlet allowed shipping and fishing activities to resume. To date, the inlet has not closed up again, but dredging is required on a regular basis to keep the waterway passable.

THE GREAT DEPRESSION

The onset of the Great Depression slowed growth and made for some lean times in the 1930s. The borough itself was at times strapped for operating cash. Throughout the 1930s, the council minutes relate the details of applications to the state for waivers and financial assistance to make ends meet. Residents of Brielle saw hard times too. A great many residents were still farmers and fishermen, but just because they could grow or catch their own food didn't mean that there were buyers for the surplus that would provide them the hard cash needed to purchase life's other necessities. Clothing, household goods, taxes and medical care were sometimes difficult to afford in those times.

Maude Goode was born in 1887 in Luray, Virginia. Little did she know that her early training as a midwife in Virginia would help her to become a vital part of the fabric of the community in Brielle, New Jersey—far off not only in distance but in time as well. While a young girl in Luray, Maude was trained as a midwife by Dr. Madison and assisted him in delivering over forty babies. In 1904, Maude married James Moon of Stanardsville, Virginia. James and Maude would become the parents of sixteen children. In 1923, the Moons settled in a house on Agnes Avenue in Brielle after living in Point Pleasant for three years.

Once in the Brielle area, Maude began working with the obstetrician Dr. Norris of Manasquan. With the coming of the Depression, many local residents could not afford a doctor to help deliver a baby. Often, if Dr. Norris could not attend to a patient, he would send Maude by herself to assist with the birth. In her years as a midwife, Maude helped bring many Brielle residents into the world.

Not content to serve only as a midwife, Maude's charity extended to many facets of the community. A quiet, unassuming woman, Maude was a champion of the poor, the homeless and the needy. She and her husband, James, maintained a large garden and canned vegetables for the winter, not only for themselves, but also to feed the poor and hungry of their community.

Reopening the inlet, the development of powerboats, the growing popularity of the automobile and Brielle's protected riverfront combined to make it the ideal spot for the new sport fishing industry to flourish. Despite the hard times brought on by the Depression, over the next few years a fleet of private fishing vessels and large party boats amassed at the docks of Brielle. Anglers flocked to Brielle from all over the world to compete in world-renowned tournaments or simply enjoy a day of fishing. A new age was dawning in Brielle—the age of sport fishing.

CHAPTER 7

THE BABY BOROUGH GROWS UP

BRIELLE: SPORT FISHING CAPITAL OF THE WORLD

Throughout the 1920s and '30s, Brielle was growing. Changes were taking place in the sport fishing industry. For centuries, men used nets to scoop up large quantities of small fish. This was fine if one were fishing for food, but at the beginning of the twentieth century a new kind of fishing emerged—sport fishing. Armed with a baited hook and line, a rod for leverage and a reel to wind up the line, sportsmen began to compete to see who could catch the biggest fish. Advances in materials and design of tackle enabled anglers to pursue bigger and bigger fish. Giant tuna and billfish were the new quarry for the new breed of angler—the big game fisherman. Though men largely dominated the sport, there were a fair number of women involved in big game fishing. The mechanical advantage given by the tackle enabled women to easily compete alongside men for the same size fish. Brielle resident Eugenie Marron was one of the most famous female anglers in history. Naturally, Brielle became a leading center for big game fishing. Many Brielle-based anglers travelled to compete in tournaments all over the world. Along with the activities of fishing itself came a burgeoning need for other support businesses and industries. Marinas, mechanics, captains and crews, restaurants and lodgings, hardware and grocery stores all flourished during the growth years.

Fishing was not always a purposeful activity—sometimes fish were caught by accident. In 1933, a giant manta ray became fouled in the anchor chain of Captain Kahn's fishing boat. At the time of the incident, captain and crew had no idea what they had captured. After the boat limped back into port, the behemoth was untangled from the chains and hauled ashore. Measuring almost twenty-two feet across and weighing eight tons, the sea monster was put on display by the Brielle Fire Company as a wonder of nature. The firefighters charged curiosity seekers ten cents per look at the beast and within six days had raised enough money to make the final payment on a

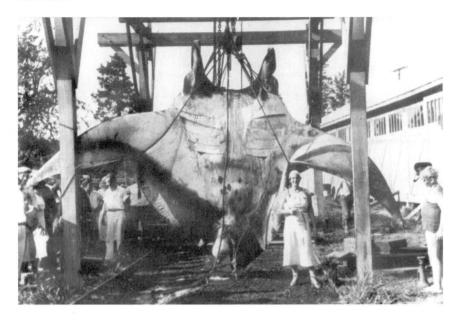

Captain Kahn's manta ray as it appeared on display at Feuerbach and Hansen's Marina.

This bait shack was constructed on pilings adjacent to the Fisk Avenue bridge on the way to Manasquan. On the right side of the photograph is where Green Avenue connects to Fisk Avenue.

new fire truck. Shortly after being hauled out, the enormous creature gave birth to several live pups. Sadly, along with their mother, the pups did not survive long. After a few days in the hot sun, the stench of the beast became unbearable and the body had to be disposed of.

Its proximity to the open ocean and miles of protected riverfront quickly established Brielle as a sport fishing mecca. The newfound popularity of the automobile in the 1920s enabled not only the wealthy to enjoy Brielle's fishing but also the new middle class. Anglers by the hundreds journeyed to Brielle each summer to try their hands at the new sport. Men and women stood shoulder to shoulder on the charter boats waiting for a tug at the end of their lines. Wealthy businessmen and professionals who owned their own boats and employed private captains made their own expeditions out into the Atlantic in search of big game fish. Sharks, giant tuna, marlin and swordfish were all brought back to the docks in Brielle. Though they did not have the notoriety of today's major sports figures, these anglers who called Brielle their home port were nevertheless titans in their field. Lou Marron and Walt McDonagh were probably the biggest names. Along with their wives, they travelled the world and fished for world records wherever they went. Not to be outdone by her husband Lou, Eugenie Marron went on to take several women's International Game Fish Association (IGFA) world records on her own, one of which still stands today.

Along with the famous, record-setting anglers, many others docked at Brielle's marinas during the golden age of sport fishing. Some were relatively obscure; others, like the couple pictured on page 106, may have been a bit more famous. There is no caption or identifying mark on the original photograph, but it has been suggested that the lady seated at the card table on this boat bears a striking resemblance to Mrs. Wallis Simpson, the American divorcée who caused a constitutional crisis in England when King Edward VIII abdicated the throne to marry her. While it may be unlikely that a former king of England and emperor of India would be sitting at a card table on a fishing boat in Brielle, New Jersey, it is known that Edward and Wallis frequented New York and Palm Beach after his abdication—towns also frequented by the Marrons and other wealthy businessmen who formed the core of the fraternity of American sport fishermen.

Businesses in Brielle grew swiftly in these formative years. Prior to the permanent opening of the Manasquan Inlet, Brielle was primarily a tourist destination and secondarily a farming community like most of the rest of Wall Township. Once tourism in the form of recreational fishing took hold, a whole new set of businesses sprouted in the area. To sustain the restaurant and tourism business, grocery and vegetable vendors set up shop

Above: The *Beachcomber* was one of the many charter boats that split time between Brielle in the summers and Florida in the winters. Many have suggested that the lady seated at the card table bears a striking resemblance to Wallis Simpson, the American divorceé who caused King Edward VIII to abdicate the British throne.

Left: Local angler Lou Marron (right) poses with his fishing guest, Harry Hulsenbeck (left), former Essex County sheriff, after a successful trip on June 29, 1936, on the *Eugenie II*. The tuna weighed in at fifty-six pounds and was their only strike of the day.

Right: Genie Marron (far left) poses on the dock of Hoffman's with her fishing party on July 8, 1936. They travelled thirty miles off Sea Girt aboard the Marrons' boat *Eugenie II* and returned with about six hundred pounds of tuna.

Below: Captain Frank Stires of the party boat *Dolphin* takes time to pose for a publicity picture about 1950. Stires's brother George was one of Brielle's young men lost in World War II, and his father, Ernest, was one of the first two candidates for tax assessor in 1919.

The Manasquan River Marlin and Tuna Club was a major sponsor of big game fishing tournaments from the 1930s through the 1960s. This early photo shows a season's worth of tournament entries hauled out of the icehouse and put on display.

Local angler Walt McDonagh's first boat was named the *Jersey Lightning*. He bought the boat used from the Laird family, owners of a local distillery. "Jersey Lightning" was a nickname for Applejack, a locally produced spirit made from cider.

here. Restaurants sprang up to cater to the influx of tourists from distant cities. Marinas and related marine service industries appeared. Through it all, older industries like crabbing and clamming remained entrenched in the fabric of daily life.

In 1938, a group of local business owners established the Brielle Chamber of Commerce. Membership was open to any individual, firm or business concerned with the general welfare and betterment of Brielle. From its inception, the chamber was both an advocacy group representing the interests of local business owners and a public relations agency for Brielle. It published maps, city directories and guidebooks to promote businesses and tourism in Brielle. The group also produced several 16 mm silent films showcasing the borough of Brielle's businesses and attractions, sport fishing activities and homes. The Brielle Chamber continues that same mission today, with the addition of charitable fundraising activities. In 2005, the chamber resurrected a popular family fishing tournament that is now held annually in June. The proceeds from the tournament are used to purchase and sink salvaged ships on the Sea Girt artificial reef just off the Manasquan Inlet.

Cook's Market was located at the intersection of Higgins Avenue and Union Avenue. Originally the intersection was in the form of a narrow *Y*, not the *T* intersection there today. The market stood on the inside crook of the *Y* and was a well-known grocery store. The business was eventually sold to Mr. A.W. Dorrer, who renamed it Dorrer's Market. The business flourished, and Dorrer was a longtime member of the Brielle Chamber. Eventually the business was sold to Maurice Holtzman, expanded and moved to Higgins Avenue in 1959 to become the Shop-Rite supermarket.

The Dinner Bell Restaurant has stood on the same site on Union Avenue since about 1931. It was built by Harold D. Edwards and was initially operated by Edwards's in-laws, Anna and Karl Grosse. It may be one of the longest-lived restaurants in Brielle, operating under several names almost continuously throughout its more than seventy-five-year history. New York Giants football player Lawrence Taylor owned and operated a bar and nightclub called LT's there in the early 1990s. The building today is home to Charlie Brown's Steakhouse and has been remodeled and expanded several times, but the silhouette of the original building is still visible today. Barbara Edwards Bacon, the builder's daughter, relates that the restaurant was well known for its homemade sausage, and customers came from miles around to purchase it. Her grandfather kept and slaughtered his own pigs on the property to make the sausage.

Moore's Vegetable Market once stood on the site of Dickson's Plumbing Supply on Union Avenue. The house in the background still stands at the corner on Agnes and Union Avenues.

John J. Morton was a local crabber who worked the waters of the Manasquan River. At the left is the old wooden bridge at Old Bridge Road.

Dickson Supply, founded in 1946 on the site of Moore's Vegetable Market, has grown from humble beginnings into an enduring and iconic Brielle institution.

Cook's Market stood at the intersection of Union Avenue and Higgins Avenue. Mr. A.W. Dorrer bought the business and operated Dorrer's Market on the same site. He sold the business to Maurice Holtzman, who joined the Shop-Rite chain in 1959 and expanded and relocated the store to Higgins Avenue in 1959.

The Dinner Bell Restaurant on Union Avenue as it would have appeared throughout the 1930s and '40s. The building has been added on to and remodeled many times, but the rounded front section is still visible in today's Charlie Brown's Steakhouse.

A menu from the Dinner Bell Restaurant, circa 1940.

This panorama of the Brielle Marina District, circa 1940s, shows Scheible's Boarding House on the left and the Brielle Inn on the right.

Before clamming became industrialized, clammers plied the waters of the Manasquan in rowboats like these. Note the "new" concrete bridge at Higgins Avenue in the background. This bridge replaced the original wooden span erected in the 1870s and served until the present Route 35 bridge was completed in 1950.

THE *MORRO CASTLE* DISASTER

The night of September 8, 1934, marked perhaps the worst maritime disaster the Brielle area has ever seen. Traveling north on its regular route between Cuba and New York, the Clyde Line steamer *Morro Castle* was south of the Manasquan Inlet when a fire suddenly broke out onboard. Fire anywhere is a serious situation, but a fire at sea is especially deadly. There is no easy escape, fire can weaken the structural integrity of a wooden hull and fuel bunkers and other flammables stored onboard can become time bombs waiting to explode. Much speculation has surrounded the cause of the fire, including the fact that the captain of the *Morro Castle* died onboard a few hours earlier under mysterious circumstances. Speculation aside, the reality was that hundreds of passengers and crew were in immediate danger, there were no established safety standards for lifesaving equipment at the time, the weather was dangerously rough and panic had rapidly set in. Passengers jumped from the burning vessel without life jackets into the rough September Atlantic. Worse yet, those who donned their life jackets prior to jumping often put themselves at greater risk. Since there were no established safety standards in the maritime industry yet, the design of those life jackets neither protected the wearer's neck and head nor did they enable the wearer to float upright when unconscious. Passengers who tried to leap to safety from the upper decks could be knocked unconscious by the impact of the ocean and would not be floated faceup by the jacket. Worse yet, some passengers' necks were snapped on impact with the ocean, killing them instantly.

Although the Jersey coast was being lashed by late summer storms that night, within a short time after receiving reports of the disaster, local mariners were among the first to respond. Rescuers and volunteers from as far north as Shark River took to the seas to search for survivors. At about 6:30 a.m. the following day, Captain John Bogan Sr. of Brielle and his sons, John Jr. and James, were at their dock in Brielle. News of the disaster had spread like wildfire, and Bogan and his sons prepared to go out to search for survivors. Bogan's boat the *Paramount* had a crew of five, and despite the fearsome weather, four of the crewmen volunteered to go out that morning. With Captain James "Speedy Jim" Bogan at the helm, they left Brielle and headed out through the Manasquan Inlet. The *Paramount* quickly encountered some rough seas; the boat was pummeled by waves crashing over the bow. The senior Bogan ordered his son to turn the ship about and head back to port. Only after John Jr. convinced his father that they were needed out there did the elder Bogan relent and order the boat turned back around. The Bogans and their crew worked tirelessly through the day in the rough seas to recover survivors and casualties alike.

The Coast Guard was also on the scene, both on the water and through an unlikely partnership with a local businessman. At this time, Brielle was also home to a small airfield, located between today's Route 70 in Brielle and Lakewood Road in Wall. Pilot and owner Matty Matelin obtained life jackets from the Coast Guard and took them aloft in his four-passenger biplane from the Brielle airfield. By the first light the next morning, dozens of survivors were still in the water, having leapt from the burning vessel without life jackets. Matty's airdropped life jackets saved dozens more lives that day. Despite the heroic efforts of all the rescuers, 134 passengers and crew perished.

The grim reality of the aftermath of the disaster was seen most clearly here in Brielle. The Bogan fleet brought survivors and casualties ashore. Survivors were quickly transported to get medical attention. The casualties were, however, a more difficult problem. Since the fire broke out at night, survivors had abandoned ship with a minimum of possessions and clothing. Bodies recovered in nightclothes and pajamas did not bear any identification. As bodies were carried ashore at Brielle, a makeshift morgue was set up on the porch of Scheible's Boarding House, which at the time adjoined Bogan's dock. Curious onlookers and, later, concerned family members flocked to Brielle to bear witness to the carnage wrought by a fire at sea.

After the last survivors had leapt toward presumed safety, after the fires had burned out and after the ship was abandoned, the *Morro Castle* continued its northerly journey, now under tow by the United States Coast Guard. The vessels continued on a northerly course, until the tow rope slackened and fouled the propeller of the Coast Guard vessel. The tow rope was cut and the *Morro Castle* continued northward, eventually running aground at Asbury Park. The burned-out hulk remained there for several months, during which throngs of curious onlookers gathered at the beach near Convention Hall to witness the aftermath of the inferno. Eventually, it was towed to New York and sold for scrap. Despite the tragedy of the *Morro Castle*, the incident brought about sweeping changes in life safety standards at sea. An investigation by the Coast Guard after the disaster revealed the shortcomings of the fatal life jacket design, and extensive changes were mandated to better ensure the safety of wearers. An investigation of the fire's path throughout the ship revealed design shortcomings that could have slowed or halted the fire's progress. Again, changes were mandated in the interior design of commercial vessels that

Fishing boat crewmen bring casualties of the *Morro Castle* disaster ashore at Bogan's dock in Brielle.

Spectators gather at the porch of Scheible's Boarding House, where a makeshift morgue had been set up for the pending identification of the *Morro Castle* dead.

An aerial view of the Brielle riverfront, looking toward Point Pleasant Beach, as it would have appeared in the late 1940s. Higgins Avenue was still the road to the bridge across the Manasquan River at this time.

would stop, or at least slow, the spread of fire onboard. Airtight and fire-resistant doors on the *Morro Castle* would have gone a long way toward saving lives that fateful night if they had only been thought of by the ship's builders.

Along with the developing tourism-based industries, real estate began to be developed in the area southwest of Higgins Avenue. The road presently known as Riverview Drive was originally called Riverview Avenue from Union Lane to Rankin Road and River Drive from Rankin Road to Old Bridge Road. Up until this time, the residential development there was confined to large summer estates belonging to wealthy New Yorkers and New Jerseyans. As Brielle fishing and tourism businesses expanded, so did opportunities for the middle class to make inroads into what was to become suburban Brielle. Little by little, residential development began to take place in the area of Riverview Drive, though it would not gain full momentum until after World War II.

CHAPTER 8

THE WAR YEARS IN BRIELLE

U pon the United States' entry into World War II on December 7, 1941, there were fewer than seven hundred full-time residents of Brielle, but the war affected them just as much as larger cities. Rationing, young men and women volunteering for the service and everyone doing his patriotic duty to contribute to the war effort were realities of daily life during wartime just as much here as everywhere else. Brielle's proximity to the coast added another threat—German U-boats regularly patrolled the waters of the East Coast. Although they did not attack us onshore, their activities disrupted daily life on the water. Tankers and freighters were sunk offshore and fishing activities were disrupted. Through it all, year-round residents and summer residents alike did what they had to do to help out with the war effort every day. The following accounts from local residents detail the daily activities on the homefront of a nation in conflict.

Summer resident Janice Felmly Wurfel recalls the following:

Knitting heavy wool sweaters for the army and navy was once an all year round practice, but it wasn't the most fun during the summer months. However, that was when we had the most time on our hands and once again we did what we could to make life more comfortable for the servicemen. Furthermore, in the '40s there was invariably a cool ocean breeze and the warmth of the wool was less objectionable. There was a lady from the Red Cross who would bring the heavy wool yarn to the Brielle Post Office on Green Avenue. She would give it to us with the sweater directions always enough yarn for a size 42 sweater. We bought our own large size wooden knitting needles. We went to the movies frequently and I would take my knitting with me. The people sitting near me would occasionally complain about the constant disturbing movement of my hands and the clicking of the needles. However when I told them I was working on a sweater for a serviceman, they were willing to put up with my effort. The next morning I would pick up stitches that I dropped while knitting in the dark. The finished products were very heavy by the time we returned them to the Red Cross lady.

Ballantine's Scotch was difficult but not impossible to get during World War II. The local market owner could and would get it in by the case for preferred customers. However, if he sold you a case of Ballantine's scotch you had to buy three cases of rum. The fifths and quarts were packaged separately in substantial cardboard boxes which were an excellent size for care packages to be sent to our servicemen. Initially when they opened the boxes they would be disappointed that they didn't contain scotch but were usually pleased to find home made candy, cookies, nuts and other non-perishable foods, a new tooth brush, toothpaste, socks, razors, scissors, Band-Aids and other small items to improve their daily existence. We frequently had gatherings when invited guests were asked to bring gifts to go in the packages. We had to drink a lot of Ballantine's to keep the care packages moving. We did what we had to do for the war effort.

If you lived near the beach your home had to have "Black Out Curtains" so light could not be seen from the sea. Cars had the top half of their headlights painted black. Gas, butter and other items were rationed and a family was issued "Gas Stamps" and "Food Stamps." Manasquan High School had air raid drills—when the sound started everyone had to leave the classroom and go stand by their locker until the "All Clear" sounded. Men too old for service volunteered to be "Air Raid Wardens."

The Coast Guard was stationed at the Fremont Hotel in Sea Girt. They held a weekly dance and girls from surrounding towns were invited. The Coast Guard patrolled the beaches at night along with their "furious" dogs. Anyone on the boardwalk was stopped and questioned while the dog was anxiously waiting for the command "attack." If you did walk on the boardwalk at night (in complete darkness) it was not unusual to see an explosion at sea. It lit up the horizon. It was either a U.S. ship had been torpedoed by a U-Boat or vice versa.

The recollections of another local family come from a lady who was ten years old in 1941. Her father was too old for the service but joined the Coast Guard Auxiliary to patrol the coast a couple of times a week in one of its boats.

She had three older brothers, one in the marines in the South Pacific, one in the Signal Corps in Alaska and the third in the Coast Guard in New York. All of their outgoing mail was censored. Service people were not permitted to reveal their whereabouts, but her marine brother developed a code whereby his father would know where he was.

Their father's name was Percy. The first letter the marine wrote was addressed to Mr. and Mrs. G. The second letter went to Mrs. and Mrs. U. and the third to Mr. and Mrs. A. When letter number four arrived, it was addressed to Mr. and Mrs. M., and the family then knew that he was stationed on Guam.

This lady remembers that if she and her friends went out for a walk or to play in the evening, they had to be home before dark because there were no streetlights. It was even too dark to go out to collect fireflies in a jar.

She also recalls that she and her mother were downtown shopping on the day the war ended. She and her mother went to the nearest church to give thanks.

There was a servicemen's canteen that was operated from 1942 to 1944 by the Brielle Unit of the American Women's Volunteer Service. During World War II, the women of Brielle and surrounding towns did their part to "keep the home fires burning."

Although many women took jobs in factories, etc., to replace the men in service, many others put their efforts into volunteering. Members of the American Women's Volunteer Service organized young people in salvaging metal and other needed materials, trained members of the community in Red Cross classes, provided motor transportation and acted as black-out wardens at night.

The Brielle unit of the American Women's Volunteer Service opened a servicemen's club on Ashley Avenue with ping pong, cards, books, games, refreshments and whatever would create a homelike atmosphere for men in our country's service. Weekly dances were held there. In December, A.W. Dorrer, owner of a local food market, donated a Christmas tree, which club members decorated. Sometimes dances were held at the Manasquan River Yacht Club.

The women in the American Women's Volunteer Service proudly wore the uniform dictated by the national organization as they went about their many duties. These women showed the world that American women were not soft and helpless but were able to contribute to the war effort to help our beloved country.

Ethyl D'Aloia Giaimo recalls the tar, formed from the diesel fuel spills of sunken ships, on the ocean and Manasquan River beaches and in the water that made a mess around the hulls of the boats. Her father paid her five dollars to clean the tar from the waterline of their boat, on which they lived all summer at the dock of the Anchorage.

Many of the older ladies rolled bandages. Melvina Kroh Maier, who was a private pilot, joined the Women's Army Corps (WAC) and ferried

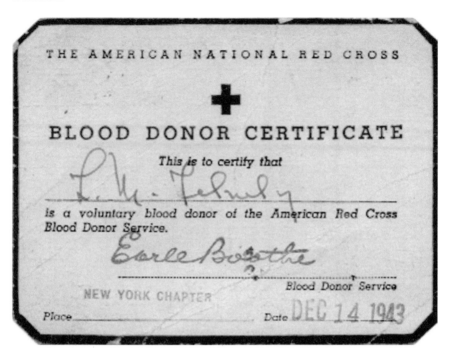

A certificate like this was given to blood donors by the Red Cross in recognition of their sacrifice during World War II.

planes all over the United States. A lot of the Brielle residents had victory gardens. You can grow anything in the sandy loam. Older men joined in civilian defense.

Once again doing their part to support the effort, many people donated blood. The blood donor certificate from the New York Chapter of the American National Red Cross specified that the person was "a voluntary blood donor of the American Red Cross Blood Donor Service." The front of the certificate included the donor's name and the original date of the donation and was signed by a member of the service. The back of the certificate stated:

> *This certificate signifies that its possessor has rendered a patriotic service by giving his or her own blood for the treatment of the seriously injured. Eight weeks must elapse between donations. When making future donations please present this certificate. Give your Blood to save a Life.*

The card included five blank lines to record the date and place.

Lifelong Brielle resident Bob Sauer recalls the following:

When I was a teenager during World War II, my bedroom was located so I had a clear view of Manasquan Inlet, of course the trees were not as large as they are now.

One night approximately 2:00 a.m. an explosion awakened me. I quickly looked out my window and I witnessed a large ball of fire offshore. I later found out that the ship now known as the Resor *wreck which eventually sank off of Barnegat was torpedoed by a German submarine. I believed the ship was a tanker owned by Esso (now Exxon).*

I used to walk the docks when I was young and if a mate did not show up I would skip school and go to work on the fishing boats. Not all boats were allowed out, only those equipped with radios so they could do double duty. Fish area patrol…one of those times I was asked by Captain Henry William owner and captain of the head boat Dolphin *if I would fish it as a mate for the day. But before we left the mate showed up late so he went instead of me. While the boat was offshore a German submarine surfaced and threatened him not to use the radio. They boarded the boat, broke his radio and stole all of the fish he had caught. They also removed most of his diesel fuel leaving him only enough to return home.*

When I was real young and I heard the roar of a fast boat coming in the inlet I would race to the River and chances are there would be a rumrunner going top speed and the Coast Guard chasing him. The Rum Runner must have had the timing just right because he would just clear the railroad bridge and the bridge tender would close the bridge for a train before the Coast Guard arrived. Makes you wonder if possibly the bridge tender had a good supply of booze.

Once in a while the rum runner did not make it in time and it was amazing how much booze ended up in all the local cellars.

The area marinas had difficult times during World War II. It was not easy for them to get gas, and it was not easy for them to get the workers they needed to service the boats. Most of the young men who were mates were in the service, and some of the younger captains were too. Skilled workers were among those who went off to war, and the marinas had to hire older men. The owners permitted private boat owners to come into the yard to work on their own boats, particularly to scrape, sand, paint and varnish. Engine problems took a long time because good mechanics were scarce and overworked. People who used pleasure craft were given gas rationing stamps

During World War II, commercial and recreational vessels were required to display markings twelve inches high for clear identification.

and frequently were able to enjoy their days on the water about half of the summer, a little longer if they saved some gas by going slower. Identification numbers on boats had to be twelve inches high by two inches wide on the port (left) and starboard (right) bows and across the top of the bow so that they were visible from land, sea and air.

The following letter was sent overseas to summer resident Lloyd Felmly by his parents at the conclusion of the war:

Brielle, N.J.
Aug 16, 1945

Dear Lloyd,
Victory. We are all dazed, even though for days we had been told it was all over. When Truman made the announcement Tuesday night at 7 everyone exploded. The celebration has been going on with variations ever since. The President declared a two-day holiday and folks took him at his word. Newark had been a madhouse all day Tuesday and became only more so that night. New York ditto. Down here everything closed up and is still closed. To us it hardly seems real. We had waited so long and despaired so often that peace seems an abnormality. War had become the accustomed way of life. Now, with gas rationing immediately lifted, fuel oil the same, blue points off most things and many other changes of atmosphere and mood, we wonder what it

will be like when we get used to it. But most of all we are thinking of you. We hope the China Theater will dissolve quickly and that you will be back in this country if not out of the service. Nancy and Puff have been down every day and Tuesday night he staged his own celebration. He rode with the Os's to Asbury Park, shouting "Daddy" and "Hurray" and waving his flag. You ask him who's coming home and he says: "Daddy". You ask him whom he'll see and he says "Puffy". You'll find him a most interesting youngster and I think he'll know you right away.

After we had recovered from the first shock we and the Bells, who came down that afternoon had a few drinks and then went up to Edith's to stay until 4 am. We started out to the Monmouth, but Al Driscoll closed all the gin mills, an excellent thing. We talked and sipped a bit and the night passed rapidly. Wednesday we all went to the ME church in Manasquan and heard Rev. C.M. Hogate deliver an inspired talk. He was a chaplain and was wounded in the last war. He was really grand. We were delighted that we went. Then we came back, had a swim and spent the rest of the day relaxing, playing bridge, etc. The Duke came down and put on a riotous show for us. He loves it here. There's so much for him to do. Nancy had dinner with us and he sat in a separate chair and ate toast, etc. He insists on coming to see us often. The other day they started for Island Heights and he raised so much hell out by the Pt. Pleasant bridge that they had to turn in and get us. We all went down to Sobey's.

I won't attempt to go into detail about how peace feels. We're trying to get used to it. I stayed up on my vacation. An editor's no good if his organization can't carry on in his absence. I was on the phone a lot though. Yesterday, however, you just couldn't get a call through. Oh, yes, here's the payoff. Anne tried to get Grandma Tuesday night and couldn't. She was worried. Yesterday the call came thru. Where do you suppose the old gal was Tues. night? Out helping blow the siren. Isn't that a riot? 76 and still going strong.

I read the Navy discharge system this am and you seem to have only 43 points of a needed 49. Could you get transferred to med school? Or is that out of the question. If I were you I'd apply for something or other. But keep your shirt on, as they say. As you wrote, it's tough on every one and in the end it will all work out for the best. As we have often said, you have the eternal consolation of having done what you thought was right. That will be with you all thru life. You can hold your head up and live with the best of them. We are your greatest admirers, let me add, although I think Puff will take no. 1 place when he sees his old gent in uniform. I tried to teach him to salute the flag down on the dock the other day. He'd say "S'ute" but

I couldn't get him to put his hand up right.

Am enclosing a few pics. The kid with Puff is Tommy Dillingham from St. Louis. Hope you have received all the mail that I know is on the way. And tell Chiang and the other Chinese to realize "there's a war off".

Love from us all.
Dad.

My Son: Here's to you and the Peace. We have won it. I hope we can keep it. We are still stunned by the sudden shock—cannot fully realize it as yet. We are so happy in a very quiet serious mood. He's wonderful. I wonder how you received the peace message what you did to celebrate. I'll bet your old daddy long legs jumped high. I would bet apprehensive though—I don't know what kind of duty you'll be called upon to do now or later on. BUT Budgie be careful. Your work is no child's play and the Japs are treacherous. You probably know little enough about their intentions etc. There will be a lot of work to be done. It would be too tragic if you should be hurt at this stage of the game. This is the second war for me—the first war in my life I waited to marry when we came home from the last war—now I am waiting for his son to come home from this war.

Today I have ordered a bond for Puffy to celebrate the end of the war. That is the best way to do it I think.

I am busy with the trees in the back—the old apple tree is cut down by the shower we are clearing the vines from the rotted lattice. The yard looks good—we took down five wild cherry trees—the apple Daddy fell from etc. Two butternut trees in the back. We are having fun with Jess and Marion Bell.

I hope you received your birthday box of cigars, cards etc.

I love you so much my darling—Take good care of yourself, too.

Daddy and I both are so happy to know now you'll be coming home.

Be Careful! Do your job well.

Love to you Lloyd dear. From Mother.

Janice is overjoyed. Marion Bell sends her love. Pictures enclosed you will love. I just won $1.13 from Pop playing Russian gin and $1.58 from Peg Costello.

Love, Mother

Honey—I love you, too! Hurry home! Nan

Many young men from the Brielle and Manasquan area answered the call of duty and went off to fight for their country during World War II. Sadly, not all of them returned home safely. The following were Brielle soldiers reported killed in action in World War II:

Robert W. Berkhofer   Nelson S. Rae
Donald R. Cooke   George Stires
Richard A. Donnelly Jr.   Willard F. Van Sickle
James B. Mills

George Stires, son of Edward and Edith Stires, enlisted in the navy prior to the United States' entry into the war. He served in the South Pacific and saw action in the Philippines during the Japanese occupation of the island nation in 1942. Stires was initially reported missing in action in May 1942 by the navy while engaged with the American Fleet in the Manila Bay area. Later, it became known that he was interred at the Japanese War Prisoner Camp #3 on Luzon Island, Philippines. Stires died at the camp on June 25, 1942.

Lifelong Brielle resident Oliver Reynolds served in the Army Air Corps during World War II. As a young man, Reynolds frequented the nearby Brielle Airfield and learned some basic aviation skills. Reynolds recalls that the airport owner, Matt Mattelin, would provide basic flight instruction to students using a "simulator" consisting of an overturned peach basket and a broomstick. Though crude, the rig demonstrated the basic operating principles of an airplane's controls. After basic training, Reynolds was stationed at Chanute Air Force Base in Illinois. During a routine training flight in Indiana, Reynolds's plane crashed, an unfortunate accident caused by a control tower error. The crash seriously injured him and one other member of the crew. The third airman in the crew was killed in the crash. After a lengthy recuperation period, Reynolds was not able to return to flight duty due to injuries sustained in the accident. After returning to duty, he was asked to volunteer for a special assignment. Despite the warning that the assignment would be dangerous and would have an expected mortality rate of 25 percent, Reynolds accepted it.

His new assignment would be as a member of one of the Army Air Corps' Floating Aircraft Maintenance Units to be deployed in the Pacific. As the Allied air forces moved westward across the Pacific, hopping from island to island, aircraft were subjected to both abuse and enemy fire. With no repair facilities on any of these tiny islands, the Army Air Corps deployed

Flags like these were displayed in mothers' windows indicating the number of sons and daughters in the service during the war. Each star represented one child. A gold star meant that a child was killed in action.

floating aircraft maintenance units aboard converted freight-passenger and Liberty ships. Each vessel was equipped with shop space, parts stores and a highly trained combat-ready crew. After a rigorous training period on the Gulf Coast, including naval training by instructors from the Great Lakes Naval Station, Reynolds and his shipmates aboard the FS-210, the SS *Colonel Oliver S. Ferson*, steamed through the Panama Canal bound for the Pacific Theatre.

Reynolds's unit was deployed late in the war but saw action on and around the islands of Guam, Saipan and Tinian. With no sign of Japanese surrender in sight, the general consensus was that a land invasion of Japan was inevitable. Most of the Allied activity in that part of the Pacific was centered on preparation and support for such an invasion. The crew of the FS-210 would have inevitably been engaged in that operation if it came to pass. For several years already, the U.S. Army had been heavily engaged in the top-secret Manhattan Project to develop and deliver an atomic bomb to an enemy target. It was hoped that the unprecedented power of this new

Brielle resident Oliver Reynolds is pictured at the far left overseeing a crash crew in action on Tinian. A B-29 bomber crashed while attempting a landing at the Tinian airfield.

weapon would bring the war to a more rapid conclusion. To that end, the island of Tinian, which was in proximity to the Japanese mainland, was chosen by the project's directors as the departure point of the 507th Bomb Group. While on Tinian, Reynolds recalls seeing the Little Boy atomic bomb being offloaded from the USS *Indianapolis* and readied for its final destination, the Japanese city Hiroshima. The *Indianapolis* also brought the second bomb, known as Fat Man, to the island at the same time. In a close brush with fate, the *Indianapolis* was torpedoed and sunk by a Japanese submarine within forty-eight hours of leaving Tinian after it delivered its classified cargo.

The army's atomic bombs dropped on Hiroshima and Nagasaki brought the war in the Pacific to a rapid conclusion. Reynolds was sent to Iwo Jima on a special repair assignment and recalls being on Iwo Jima at the time of the Japanese surrender. After the Japanese surrender, the *FS-210* departed Tinian, and Reynolds remained on the island, serving as supervisor of the Air Drone Crash Crew. In February 1946, Reynolds sailed home from Saipan and returned safely to Brielle.

CHAPTER 9

SUBURBAN BRIELLE TAKES HOLD

After World War II, widespread travel by automobiles on highways expanded the reach of the American people. Previously thought of as being out in the country, Brielle was suddenly not quite so far away from the city.

Throughout the 1940s and '50s, Brielle, just like many other towns in America, was completing a transformation from a country farm outpost into a suburb. Brielle experienced a population surge during this time period, requiring the construction of a new school building in 1954. The library was expanded in 1953 and moved to the basement of the old school building. The police department and borough offices were relocated there as well in 1959. That move required a substantial refit of the building from its first life as a school. That same population surge spurred the development of new housing on the locations of now abandoned farms and large estates that were being subdivided into smaller residential lots.

Roads continued to be improved and expanded, firmly linking Brielle to other parts of the state. In 1934, State Route 70 came to Brielle, complete with a new drawbridge over the Manasquan River. This new span replaced the old wooden swing bridge at Old Bridge Road that had seen over one hundred years of service. This bridge linked the southwestern side of Brielle, now being developed at a rapid pace, to the still rural areas of Point Pleasant and Brick.

As some roads were being improved, others were deteriorating. In 1946, a section of the Route 35 bridge over the Manasquan River at Brielle suddenly and without warning collapsed. Motorists were stranded on the span, and local boaters hastened to rescue them. Images of the cars stranded mid-span were memorialized in the media—a popular picture features the automobile of local resident and businessman Harry Sauer abandoned just feet from the broken span. The span was hastily repaired, and the state began to draw up plans to replace the old bridge with a newer, larger span. The new plans

The Brielle School boys' baseball team poses for a picture outside the school, circa 1947. The greenhouses across the street were part of a commercial farm at the location of the present Route 35 North offramp.

Dedication day at the new Brielle Elementary School in 1954. Principal Myron Turner is standing at the right of the crown in the light-colored jacket. This school was built on a portion of the old Rankin farm.

The new Route 70 bridge over the Manasquan River as it appeared in the late 1940s. The Brainard estate is still visible in the upper right. That estate was subdivided to build the development on the King's Path.

called for a complete replacement of the bridge and realignment of the highway about 150 yards to the east. Many properties were lost to the project and not regained, since the old Higgins Avenue approach to the bridge was left *in situ*. One notable property was fortunately moved instead of being demolished. This is the old Scheible's Boarding House on Ashley Avenue. The three-story structure was lifted off its foundation, rotated 180 degrees and moved several hundred feet northwest to its present location in 1949.

The fishing fleet experienced some sluggish times during the war due to threats of U-boat patrols offshore; scarcity of gasoline, metals and other vital materials; and the fact that the navy sometimes commandeered fishing boats. Once we returned to peacetime, the industry picked right up where it had left off and continued a period of rapid growth. Big game fishing tournaments attracted a wide spectrum of participants; postwar prosperity brought more small, private boats to Brielle. Some of the large party boats were actually converted war surplus vessels. Dynasties of fishing families arose in Brielle—the Bogans, the Chapmans, the Shirleys, the Pharos, the Zubers and the Sevastakis—and more operated fleets of party boats catering to thousands of visitors.

BIG GAME FISHERMEN OF BRIELLE

Local residents and tourists alike continued to bring fishing fame to Brielle. Not all of the fishing took place from the docks of Brielle, but the anglers nonetheless drew the attention back to Brielle and continued its reputation as the Sport Fishing Capital of the World. Lou Marron and his wife and fishing partner, Eugenie, split their residence between New York and Brielle, later adding Palm Beach to the list. The Marrons were world-renowned anglers, socialites and philanthropists but were still "regular Brielle people," popular with both young and old. The Marrons' parties and social gatherings at their Brielle homestead *Riverbend* on Crescent Drive were lavish affairs, with guest lists that included luminaries like General Douglas MacArthur, New Jersey governor Alfred E. Driscoll and their big game fishing comrades, as well as their neighbors from Brielle. Though they had no children of their own, "Uncle Lou," as the youngsters of the area knew him, was a dashing heroic figure equal to Mickey Mantle. Their fame was such that they attracted the sponsorship of, and became the endorsers of, major fishing tackle manufacturers like Ashaway fishing line and Chrysler marine engines. Throughout his fishing career, Lou was said to have owned more than fifteen fishing boats, half of them named *Eugenie*. The *Eugenie VIII*, which he had built by Morton Johnson's shipyard in Bay Head in 1957, was well documented in a feature article in *Sports Illustrated* magazine. Always the philanthropist, when he was through with the boat around 1960, he donated it to the Woods Hole Oceanographic Institute in Massachusetts for use as a research vessel.

Both Marrons travelled the world with an elite fraternity of big game fishermen. They didn't just fish for sport though; the Marrons also fished for science. Through a partnership with the University of Miami, Lou sponsored several expeditions to the Pacific Coast of South America to study marine life. In addition to documenting the life cycle of the broadbill swordfish, they collected a wealth of oceanographic data and studied the elusive giant squid. Since there are many similarities between the nervous systems of squid and humans, many samples of squid neurons were shipped by air back to research laboratories at the Massachusetts Institute of Technology (MIT) to help scientists better understand how the human nervous system works. While on these expeditions in the 1950s, Lou and Genie both set IGFA world records for broadbill swordfish. Lou landed a 1,152-pound broadbill on 130-pound test line that still stands today. Genie's 772-pound broadbill remains the women's all-tackle record.

World-famous Brielle angler Lou Marron poses here with his world record 1,152-pound broadbill swordfish, caught on May 7, 1953, off the coast of Chile. Marron's record with the IGFA still stands today. The mounted fish remains on display at the Miami Road and Reel Club in Miami, Florida.

Both Lou and Eugenie Marron were celebrities in the fishing world and were sought after to endorse fishing-related products. Here they appear in an ad for Chrysler marine engines.

Above: The *E-Z* was one of several popular party boats moored at Zuber's Basin in Brielle. George Sevastakis, who later served Brielle as a councilman, is seen here at the helm.

Left: Mr. and Mrs. Walt McDonagh fishing together aboard the *Jersey Lightning*.

THE BIRTH OF SUBURBAN BRIELLE

Brielle's growth never slowed or looked back in the 1950s and '60s. The completion of the Garden State Parkway in 1957 connected Brielle to the metropolitan centers of northern New Jersey and New York City in an entirely new way. Within a span of a few years, automobile access was easy, and commuting to work many miles away became a way of life for millions of Americans. With this new lifestyle came an increasing demand for housing in the suburbs. The last of the farmlands and large estates in the western section of town in the hills past the golf course were being sold off and subdivided. New streets were laid out, branching off River Drive, which by now was known as Riverview Drive, all the way to Higgins Avenue.

Just as development accelerated on the west side of Brielle, it did on the east side as well. It was not as obvious there since many lots had already been developed and the existing lots that had been laid out were smaller. There were no large estates to clear in that part of town. Howell Drive was cut through from Union Lane to Route 35, and a tract of homes was built there. The marina area on the riverfront was still bustling with charter boats and private vessels alike. The big hotels and resorts were long gone, but a small boardinghouse or motel industry had grown up around the fishing fleet. The large home at the corner of Union Avenue and Union Lane was one such venture. These businesses provided a valuable support service for the charter boat industry. Fishermen would travel to Brielle the night before going out, spend the night at a boardinghouse and be ready to sail first thing the next morning. Another boardinghouse was located on Ashley Avenue across from Zuber's marina, now the Brielle Landing condominiums. That boardinghouse was run by Mary Keigher, wife of Captain Donald Keigher, who moored his boat across the street. This was certainly a convenient arrangement for a weekend fisherman without a house at the shore.

With Brielle's development into a suburban community came an influx of new families with children, but children were certainly nothing new to Brielle. To that end, along with providing essential municipal services for their parents, the governing body of Brielle had for many years already funded a program known as the Brielle Playground. This was the forerunner to today's Recreation Commission and provided safe and constructive activities for schoolchildren in the summer months. Though funded by the borough and private contributions, the Brielle Playground was also endorsed by the school and conducted many programs utilizing the school facilities and grounds. Along with these locations, the Brielle Playground also maintained and staffed a sandy beach on the eastern edge of town, accessible from East

Magnolia Avenue. Bathers there were able to enjoy the calm, protected waters of the Glimmer Glass. Besides being a popular recreational spot, the Brielle Playground also conducted swimming lessons there.

Manasquan Brielle Little League was founded in 1953, with David J. Brown and Francis G. White as principal organizers. The program included boys ages eight to twelve from Brielle, Manasquan, Sea Girt and a portion of Wall. A total of 155 boys turned out for tryouts; four teams were uniformed and equipped. The organization obtained its franchise from the National Little League headquarters at Williamsport, Pennsylvania.

In 1954, through the Borough of Manasquan, ground was procured for a field at the north end of Second Avenue. With the help of many individuals, a field house and clubhouse were built. A girls' league was formed in 1974.

THE CHURCH IN BRIELLE

Up until the late 1950s, Brielle was the holder of a peculiar record. Cited at one time by Robert L. Ripley as a town with sixteen bars and no churches, in the summer of 1955, a group of local residents concerned about the lack of a church in their community began to formulate plans to change that. Through the involvement of Dr. Norman Vincent Peale, the Reformed Church in America was quickly identified as being interested in founding a congregation here. The Church in Brielle was formally organized on March 3, 1957, and the congregation held its first service at Brielle Elementary School on that date. By April, the parcel of land at the corner of Riverview Drive and Rankin Road had been acquired. Soon after, a building committee was formed, retained an architect and instructed him to develop plans for a church building. The committee directed that he should keep in mind the beauty of simplicity, such as was found in early New England churches. By 1958, the building was complete, and the new church had installed as its first pastor Reverend Lynn Joosten. A notable distinction for this building is that it featured the first all-fiberglass steeple. Soon afterward, the Christian Education Building was constructed to provide classroom and meeting space. After a period of further growth in membership, the sanctuary was enlarged and connected with the school building in 1968. The Church in Brielle is also noted for its Nursery School for children ages three to five. The school serves children from Brielle and all of the surrounding communities. The church's participation in the fabric of the community extends to Scouting as well. Since 1956, the church has been the chartering organization for Brielle Cub Scout Pack 63.

New and innovative businesses were coming to Brielle at that time also. The passenger ferry *Cranford*, which was used daily by commuters traveling from North Jersey to New York City, had been recently retired from service. Some investors bought the vessel in 1962 and towed it to Brielle, with the intent to permanently moor the ferry at a dock and convert it into a restaurant. It was to be located at the site of the old Brielle Inn, which had recently closed. All went according to plan until it was time for the boat to transit the relatively narrow railroad bridge opening. Either the ferry was too wide for the opening or the opening was too narrow for the ferry. In either case, the boat collided with the bridge structure and caused considerable damage to both. The ferry did finally make it through and was moored at its final location. The damage to the ferry was repaired as part of its refit into a restaurant. The damage to the railroad bridge was a bit more problematic. As a result of the accident, the bridge was rendered inoperable for several weeks. The disruption of train service was a burden to the regular commuters on the line. Service stopped in Manasquan, and the trains simply reversed direction on the track since the only turnaround on the line was at the southern terminus in Bay Head. Commuters bound for Point Pleasant Beach and Bay Head would disembark in Manasquan and were transported by bus to their final destinations. Likewise, buses ran from the southern stations to Manasquan in the mornings.

The restaurant was a successful venture for many years. It eventually closed in the 1980s, when the marina where the boat was moored was sold to a developer. The *Cranford* found yet a third life as a piece of submerged wreckage on the Sea Girt artificial reef off the coast of Manasquan. Rather than risk a repeat of the entry of the ferry into Brielle, state and railroad agencies insisted that the hull be stripped completely of all extraneous parts to be certain that it would clear the opening.

For many years, Brielle residents relied on the Manasquan First Aid Squad for medical emergencies. In 1962, a group of community-minded volunteers organized the Brielle First Aid Squad to service the emergency needs of residents. In 1967, after many years of dedicated fundraising, the present First Aid Squad building was completed and dedicated. An addition to that building was added a few years later, providing additional meeting and rental hall space.

With the United States' entry into the conflict in Vietnam, young men of Brielle were called to the service of their country. One such young man was Specialist Four Carl Foster, United States Army. Foster was a rifleman and grenadier with the Thirty-fifth Infantry, Second Battalion, Company B. While on a reconnaissance patrol in the jungles of Vietnam on the night

The Jersey Central Railroad commuter ferry *Cranford* as it appeared upon its arrival at the Brielle dock that it would call home for the next nineteen years.

Brielle Beach along the Glimmer Glass was a popular local recreational spot throughout the 1950s and '60s. The natural shoreline is primarily mud and silt—the sand had to be trucked onto the site and continually replenished.

Underhill Pontiac was another iconic Brielle business at the corner of Riverview Drive and Higgins Avenue. Here the new 1962 models are showcased.

Lenzen's Brielle Pharmacy opened at the corner of Riverview and Higgins, diagonally opposite Underhill Pontiac, in 1966. This Brielle institution remained for almost forty years, until the building was sold and subdivided into smaller stores.

In the 1960s, the Brielle Chamber of Commerce sponsored a Christmas home decorating contest. Here, chamber president Ray Haggeman poses with some girls from Brielle School who made posters advertising the contest.

As with today's Pride of Brielle award, the Brielle Chamber of Commerce has always recognized individuals and organizations for exemplary community service. Here, at the 1967 Christmas dinner, Neil Lomax (center) accepts the community service award on behalf of the Brielle First Aid Squad from outgoing President John Bogan III (left).

of February 8, 1967, Specialist Foster slipped into a concealed waterhole and drowned. Foster was posthumously awarded the Purple Heart and the Bronze Star for his meritorious service and valor in combat. Foster's death made his mother, Doris Foster, Brielle's youngest Gold Star mother and the recipient of a special award by the Gold Star Mothers Club. After Foster's death, the Buchanan-Foster-Stone Veterans of Foreign Wars (VFW) Post 10103 was founded in Brielle. In addition to Foster, the post's namesakes included George Buchanon, a U.S. Navy veteran of World War I, and Dee W. Stone, also killed in Vietnam. Previously, there was not much black representation in the VFW, and the establishment of this post was a historic event for Brielle. Post 10103 also had a Women's Auxiliary, which became a great charitable fundraising organization within the town. Aside from assisting the post with Buddy Poppy sales and placing flags on the graves of veterans, the women distributed baskets for the needy and raised the funds for and presented the Brielle First Aid Squad with its first heart monitor. By the late 1970s, membership in the post waned and it became inactive. The Women's Auxiliary continued its activities for a few more years, but by 1984 it, too, had disbanded.

CHAPTER 10

FIFTY YEARS AND BEYOND

In 1969, Brielle celebrated a significant milestone—its fiftieth anniversary of incorporation. Dozens of dedicated residents joined together to form committees to plan the yearlong celebration. Dinner dances, parades, golf and fishing tournaments, contests and yachting regattas were planned and executed. Dignitaries and special guests participated in all facets of the ceremonies. Coincidentally, at the same time Brielle found itself with some unexpected celebrities in town—Brielle residents Colonel and Mrs. Edwin Aldrin Sr. Their son Edwin "Buzz" Aldrin Jr. became the second man to walk on the moon on July 20, 1969. Though not technically a Brielle resident, Aldrin visited his parents and sister here frequently. In an interesting foreshadowing of Buzz's future career, Aldrin's mother Marion's maiden name was Moon.

Brielle's growth continued steadily throughout the years before and after the fiftieth anniversary. Real estate development continued on the southwest side of town. Large tracts of vacant land were sold off and subdivided into suburban developments, mainly in the area surrounding Birch Drive. Houses sprang up on the part of the old Rankin farm adjacent to Rankin Road and in the vicinity of Shore Drive and Cedar Lane. Expansion and growth took a toll on the municipal services and the school system as well. In the late 1960s, school overcrowding was at such a state that the Board of Education tried to finance the construction of an addition to the building to accommodate the growth. The referendum failed the first time around. Temporary classroom trailers on the south side of the school property adjacent to the present-day municipal parking lot were employed to alleviate the overcrowding. The borough offices at the time were located in the present-day building, but some free space there was also used for overflow classroom space. Likewise, some classes were held in the Curtis House across the street. In 1969, the district again tried a bond referendum to raise the funds to expand. At that time, a group of concerned citizens formed the KIDS (Kommittee for

This fiftieth-anniversary commemorative stained-glass piece was designed by anniversary committee chairman George Goodfellow and executed in Switzerland. Only three are known to exist.

Informed Decision on our School) to raise awareness about the district's needs. This time the referendum passed by a two-to-one margin, and soon after ground was broken for the addition to the existing school building. The expansion added eleven classrooms, a gymnasium, a library and an art room. The expansion would carry the facility through to the next period of population growth twenty-five years later.

The year 1973 marked the founding of the Union Landing Historical Society in Brielle. Carole A. Clarke, who would later become the first borough historian, and Judy Gardner began formulating plans for a local historical society to document and preserve the area's rich history. Earlier in

Because of overcrowding, the school was forced to use temporary classroom trailers beginning in the 1968–69 school year. The trailers were placed in the ball field adjacent to the borough hall parking lot.

In September 1969, ground was broken for the first addition to the Brielle School. Pictured here (left to right) are Marguerite (Peg) Beckett, board secretary; Frederick Lombard, board attorney; Edward Pavlovsky, principal; Myron Taylor, board president; David Pease, project architect; George Wall, board vice-president; and Edward O'Sullivan, electrical contractor.

the year, the pair had been appointed by the Brielle Council to be chairman and secretary of the town's bicentennial committee. A group of like-minded citizens joined with Clarke and Gardner to move the project forward. They envisioned an organization that would provide educational opportunities for the community, preserve and document the past with the establishment of a museum and provide a social organization for local history enthusiasts. The first officers elected were Mr. Clarke as president, Mrs. Gardner as secretary, Mrs. Hugo V. Dzenis as vice-president and Mrs. Richard L. Scott as treasurer. The society's first trustees were Councilman George Goodfellow, Dr. Peter J. Guthorn and Mrs. George Mohlman. Mrs. Mohlman first came to the area as Miss Grace Dalrymple in 1901. Mrs. Mohlman proposed the name Union Landing Historical Society to memorialize one of the names by which the region was first known and one that had defined its identity for many years. From its first informal meeting in February 1973, the society has grown into a dedicated group of individuals actively engaged in recording our history for generations to come.

BRIELLE DAY

Local lore states that "it never rains on Brielle Day," and since the first Brielle Day on September 8, 1973, that maxim has remained reasonably true. Brielle Day is always the first Saturday after Labor Day and was conceived by Councilman (later Mayor) Robert Collinson. Mr. Collinson's idea was to create a sort of "community day" event in which all of the town's organizations could participate and from which they could benefit either financially or aesthetically. The date was chosen to be after school was in session to ensure that there would be a substantial local turnout, since the event was initially targeted toward residents. Nonprofit organizations, including the Women's Club, Fire Company, First Aid Squad, Union Landing Historical Society, Boy and Girl Scouts, Garden Club and Riverview Seniors, are major participants in the event. These groups stage special events and operate food and drink concessions to raise money for themselves and reinforce the tremendous sense of community that has always existed here in Brielle. A now extensive craft fair that features dozens of crafters and artisans joins these core groups. The Union Landing Historical Society originally hosted the fair, but in later years the Brielle Woman's Club has taken charge of the craft portion of the activities. What began in 1973 as a primarily local event now attracts over twenty thousand attendees each year. Early Brielle Days traditionally began with a parade through town, with games, craft vendors plying their

Fifty Years and Beyond

The first few Brielle Days began with a parade through town. Today, the event begins with the popular Brielle Day Hill and Dale Race.

Mayor Robert Collinson, founder of Brielle Day, poses with the 1978 committee and a commemorative T-shirt.

wares and food concessions open for business at Brielle Park throughout the afternoon. In later years, the start of Brielle Day was marked by the 9:00 a.m. running of the Brielle 5K/10K Hill and Dale Race. Runners from all over the tri-state area come to Brielle each year for this well-known race through the "hills and dales" of the country club section of Brielle, west of Higgins Avenue.

BRIELLE PARK AND THE CURTIS HOUSE

It wasn't always there, but today a central feature in the geography of Brielle is Brielle Park. The park, sometimes incorrectly called Green Acres Park, sits on a parcel of land bordered by Union Lane, South Street, Legg Place and the far western portion of Harris Avenue that is not passable by automobiles.

149

Brielle

Purchased with the help of federal Green Acres funds (from which it obtained its popular nickname) in the late 1960s/early 1970s, that area was home to the last thriving agricultural industry in Brielle—commercial flower farming. Fred Curtis was the last owner/operator of such a venture in Brielle. His farm encompassed several acres in the vicinity of his family's homestead, now one of the few remaining buildings on the Brielle Park tract. Curtis's house is a white, two-story frame dwelling fronting Union Lane. The house is believed to have been built in the early twentieth century, based on its architecture and design features. No one is really sure of the exact date, nor is it recorded anywhere. We do know that the original house had three bedrooms, a kitchen, living room, dining room and a small basement. It is likely that the basement was used for storage of food prior to the advent of mechanical refrigeration. The original basement was not even a full basement—it was only in the center area under the house. The left and right sides were constructed as a Yankee basement, just a short crawlspace under the main floor that provided some dead air space for insulation. At some time after the house was built, one of the upstairs bedrooms was converted into an indoor bathroom. One can still see today the tiles applied over the original walls, complete with cutout areas for a sink, bathtub, toilet and water heater.

Fred Curtis and his wife lived in the family homestead until their deaths. Upon Fred's death in 1964, title to the house passed to his niece Dorothy. She sold the house and several adjoining lots to the Borough of Brielle for the sum of $21,500, quite a lot of money in those days. Once the property was acquired, the wheels were set in motion for the development of the area for the benefit of all Brielle residents. The house was converted into a community meeting and activity venue and was even, for a time, used as an overflow space for crowded Brielle School classrooms in the late '60s and early '70s. Once funds became available for the purchase of surrounding land under the Green Acres Program, trees were cleared, ball fields built and existing houses demolished. Aside from the Curtis House, one other structure was spared the wrecking ball. A small, Dutch Colonial house was offered for sale by the borough for the sum of $1. The only condition was that the buyer had to remove the house from the future park site. That house was purchased under those terms, moved and still stands today at 704 Schoolhouse Road. In 1978, the construction of an additional large meeting room to the west side of the Curtis House was completed, expanding the house into its present form. A few years later, the remnants of the Loughran Gardens retail showroom, one of the few remaining original buildings on the site, was renovated and converted into the present Brielle Public Library.

As the 1970s progressed, Brielle continued to grow as a community but also began to change. The sport fishing and charter boat industry that had dominated the early years began to wane. Perhaps it was overfishing, or perhaps it was part of the inevitable ebb and flow of the population of marine life, but the scarcity of fish in the Sport Fishing Capital of the World did not bode well for the charter fishing business. Boats stopped sailing, marinas began to close and the business landscape of Brielle changed again. Areas that had formerly been marine commercial districts were rezoned into condominium developments. Restaurants and retail shops continued to thrive but were forced to rely more heavily on local residents rather than the tourist trade. Many marine businesses simply closed and sold off their properties to developers during this time, but one notable exception was the Bimini Yacht Club. Located on the northern end of Ashley Avenue, the Bimini was a posh restaurant and nightclub for most of its storied history. Notable celebrities, including Johnny Carson, frequented the club.

On the evening of December 2, 1976, a fire broke out in the still occupied restaurant. Battling the frigid temperatures, as well as the blaze, firefighters from five neighboring towns responded and worked early into the morning to control the fire. Brielle firefighter Ed Convery was instrumental in rescuing several patrons trapped on the second floor of the restaurant. Convery was subsequently cited for bravery by the department for his heroic actions to save lives that night. Once destroyed by fire, the management elected not to rebuild the club, and another Brielle institution was lost.

The 1990s brought another period of population growth to Brielle and with it overcrowding in the school. The 1970 expansion had served the people of Brielle well over the last twenty or so years, but demand for space and the need for technological improvements pushed the Brielle School District

This was the scene the morning after the fire at the Bimini Yacht Club. There were no life-threatening injuries, but the famous nightclub and restaurant was completely destroyed.

to another chapter in its expansion. Led by grass-roots community support again, the district went out for a bond referendum to build a third addition onto the 1954 school building. This time, the referendum was passed on the first try and ground was broken in 1999.

THE OSBORN FAMILY BURIAL GROUND

By the last quarter of the twentieth century, a ride up or down Holly Hill Drive would have revealed a small forested and overgrown area at the curve in the road. A cast-iron signpost now identifies this as the location of the historic Osborn Family Burial Ground, although not long ago this graveyard was barely noticeable from the road. Members of the Union Landing Historical Society, many community residents and others in Monmouth County had become increasingly concerned over the continuing deterioration of this ancient graveyard (with twenty-one known burials between 1822 and 1868). It was feared that this bit of heritage and history was in danger of disappearing forever if some action was not taken. One of the graves contains the remains of Revolutionary War soldier Lieutenant Abraham Osborn, upon whose farm this burial ground was established. Decades earlier, the Longstreet Graveyard had been lost to "progress," as indeed have many throughout the county and state. It would have been contrary to the society's mission not to save, protect and secure the last one.

The mission statement proposal identified a goal to restore and preserve a site of local historic importance and to utilize that proposed experience to stimulate public interest in, and help further an understanding and appreciation of, our local heritage. In addition, the project would serve to reestablish respect and restore a sense of quiet dignity for this too long neglected final resting place of departed members of a once prominent local family. Authorization to embark on this task came from Chapter 294, Laws of 1983, sections C.40:10B-1 through C.40A:4-45,18. This law, the Historic Cemeteries Act, noted that

> *many historic cemeteries have fallen into disrepair, disorder and decay. The legislature, therefore, declares that it is altogether fitting and proper, and in the public interest, to enable local governmental units to assist in the restoration, maintenance and preservation of such cemeteries.*

Upon request, the Borough of Brielle promptly and generously offered to assist in the restoration.

The first task was to locate and identify all boundary markers. Local surveyor Charles O'Malley generously handled this undertaking for the society as a community service. The first part of the borough's assistance included extensive help from the Department of Public Works, handling tree and underbrush removal. This was accomplished with exemplary cooperation from Tom Nolan, borough administrator; Bill Burkhardt, superintendent of public works; and Bob McArthur, assistant superintendent. The society contracted with Falkinburg Tree Experts to remove seven large trees. All work was supervised by project director John Belding, who at that time was also the Union Landing Historical Society president.

Once the land was cleared, the complexity of the remainder of the task became apparent. Every gravestone, with the exception of the one that marked the grave of Lieutenant Osborn, was partially or completely broken, some in as many as six fragments. Most were scattered, and many pieces were buried or missing. The challenge was to attempt to match up the broken pieces and then attempt to identify the original location of each remaining headstone and footstone. It developed that virtually all of the stones had been broken off at ground level, or just below, and over the years almost all had been covered by soil and were no longer visible. By good fortune, most of the broken off sub-terra pieces were still upright in the ground. As they were located, each in-ground stone was made plumb and then it was determined which grave it represented. Fortunately, Ernest Reed had reaffirmed an inventory in 1945, and this resource was available. While he did not use a numbering system or draw a map, he did list the graves in order. Prior to reattaching all broken sections, it had to be determined that all pieces fit together perfectly to form a single gravestone. All pieces from the headstones of eighteen of the twenty-one graves were cemented together with epoxy cement. The final three required more reconstruction work as significant pieces were missing.

While probing for buried stones, an old foundation of brick and mortar, not listed in any graveyard inventory, was discovered in the exact center of the burial ground. This foundation measured three feet by three feet by two feet deep. It is assumed that this may have been the foundation for some type of monument that had been removed years ago, if indeed it had ever been completed. The bricks used are of an antique variety, possibly manufactured locally.

As restoration progressed, the society erected an iron fence around the perimeter of the burial ground. The fence provides site security and makes a visual statement of the existence of this historic site. For aesthetic qualities, black wrought iron of mid-nineteenth-century design was chosen.

After the Union Landing Historical Society's extensive rehabilitation project in 2001, the Osborn Family Burial Ground was returned to its original idyllic appearance. The society hosts an annual Decoration Day observance there each May.

Also erected was a map board, placed to the right of the gate, showing the location of all of the graves, including headstone inscriptions. The bricks in the walkway leading to the gate were acquired in 2002 from the demolished Manasquan Borough Hall. That building had originally been erected as a school in 1880.

Those buried here include Lieutenant Osborn and his wife, Elizabeth, as well as the three wives of their son James—Elizabeth, Hannah and Jane—all of whom died at an early age. In addition, thirteen of James's children are buried here, ranging from age one day through childhood and young adulthood. There are also three relatives buried here: Elias Burge, age eleven, and James and Jane Goble. The Gobles lived on what is now Ramshorn Drive in Wall. In July 2002, the society contracted with USRadar to conduct a ground radar inspection of the graveyard to determine whether there were any unmarked graves. Seven were located and marked. It is believed that one is the grave of James and another a married daughter, Catherine Elizabeth Osborn Collins. Two of the five other unmarked graves are believed to be the original burial locations of Elizabeth Borden and Charlotte Borden, whose remains were disinterred and moved to a family mausoleum at the new Greenwood Cemetery on November 4, 1902. The three other graves remain a mystery at this time.

After the completion of the first phase of the project, the borough's physical and financial assistance continued. In 2006, a gas lantern was installed by the Public Works Department on the site. Then, in 2008, the Water Department installed a water spigot to assist in maintaining the plantings on the site.

EPILOGUE

Like many other New Jersey towns, the population and general character of Brielle have experienced a steady ebb and flow throughout the years. Unlike many others, Brielle's changes have always been both positive and productive. There was never an industry or manufacturer that left the area with an economic void and created a ghost town. Brielle and its residents have always made the cycles of change work for them in a positive manner. As each generation grows up and moves away, more young people follow in their wake. Some families have remained here for decades, each succeeding generation continuing to enjoy the experiences offered by life at the Jersey Shore in Brielle. Brielle's population has experienced a steady growth in recent decades, and each generation does its part to add to the quality of life in Brielle. The sense of community under which Brielle was created by the original developers has never left us.

BIBLIOGRAPHY

Allen, Colonel Ethan. "Monmouth Hero of the Revolution." *Journal of American History* (1910). Reprint, Shore Press, January 23, 1910.

Archives of New Jersey. Abstracts of Wills, 1793.

Archives of the State of New Jersey. 2nd Series, Vol. II. "Extracts from American Newspapers, 1778." Edited by Francis B. Lee. 1903.

———. 2nd Series, Vol. III. "Newspaper Extracts 1779." Edited by William Nelson. 1906.

Asbury Park Evening Press, June 7, 1919.

Asbury Park Press, October 1970; March 23, 1986.

Belding, John E. "History of Boxwood Cottage." Research paper donated to the Union Landing Historical Society, 1987.

Bretton Woods Community Directory. 1941.

Brielle 50th Anniversary Book. Brielle, NJ: 1969.

Brown, James S. *Allaire's Lost Empire*. Freehold, NJ: Transcript Printing House, 1938.

———. Article about saltworks. *Asbury Park Press*, April 2, 1978.

———. *Remember Old Monmouth*. Bicentennial Publication of the Monmouth County Board of Chosen Freeholders in cooperation with the *Asbury Park Press*, n.d.

Clarke, Carole A. "Bicentennial Briefs" column. *Coast Star*, 1974–1980.

———. "Then and Now." In *The History of Brielle: Union Landing Revisited*. Brielle, NJ: Union Landing Historical Society Inc., 1989.

———. Two Union Salt Works articles. *Coast Star*, March 15 and 22, 1979.

Coast Star, September 8, 1922; December 16, 1976; March 8, 1984; July 25, 1985; January 22, 1987; April 23, 1987; April 30, 1987.

Correspondence from President Bancroft Gheradi, August 29, 1933.

Craven, Wesley Frank. *New Jersey and the English Colonization of North America*. Princeton, NJ: D. Van Nostrand Co. Inc., 1964.

Declaration of Abraham Osborn in order to obtain his pension, 1832. Copy provided by Jeffrey C. Osborn.

BIBLIOGRAPHY

Errikson, Sarah R. "History of Manasquan." N.p., n.d.

Fiftieth Anniversary Booklet. Brielle, NJ: Brielle's Fiftieth Anniversary Booklet Committee, 1969.

Files of Brielle borough historian John Belding.

Freehold Democrat. Monmouth County Historical Association archives.

"General Rules and Regulations of the Gerlach Academy." Pamphlet.

"Gerlach Academy, Brielle, N.J." Brochure, 1906.

Green Family Records

Guthorn, Peter J. "Life Along the Manasquan River." In *The History of Brielle: Union Landing Revisited.* Brielle, NJ: Union Landing Historical Society Inc., 1989.

————. *The Sea Bright Skiff & Other New Jersey Shore Boats.* New Brunswick: Rutgers University Press, n.d.

Hendricks, Patricia Kroh. "Pearce's Boatyard" and "The Post Office on Green Avenue." In *The History of Brielle: Union Landing Revisited.* Brielle, NJ: Union Landing Historical Society, Inc., 1989.

Hess, William M.E. *On History's Trail.* Vol. II, Book 4, "The Jersey Coast." New York: Pageant-Poseidon Ltd., 1976.

"History of Boxwood Cottage." Union Landing Historical Society.

History of Howell: Alma Danahay and her 8th Grade Class of 1967. Reprint, Howell Historical Society, 1982.

History of Manasquan. Manasquan, NJ: Manasquan National Bank, 1950.

"The History of Monmouth County New Jersey." Ellis.

Holmquist, Helen D. *The Brielle Story.* N.p.: Privately printed, 1961.

Holmquist, Natalie R. "Early Settlers and the Revolution"; "The Union Salt Works"; "Union Landing Sea Captains;" and "Early Hotels and Restaurants." In *The History of Brielle: Union Landing Revisited.* Brielle, NJ: Union Landing Historical Society Inc., 1989.

Horner, William S. *This Old Monmouth of Ours.* Freehold, NJ: Moreau Bros., 1932.

Jones, Margaret Mac Kellar. Article on Abraham Osborn. Submitted to the Union Landing Historical Society, 1987.

Kell, Jean B. *Our Neighboring Village of Allaire.* Printed in USA, 1958.

Kneeley, Anita M. Paper written for the Brielle Board of Education, Brielle, New Jersey.

Kraft, Herbert C. *An Archaeological Reexamination and Evaluation of a Prehistoric Indian Site at Brielle, Monmouth County, New Jersey.* N.p.: Seton Hall University, 1975.

Kroh, Ananette L. Article. *Leader,* June 28, 1956.

Kull, Irving S. *New Jersey, A History.* Vols. I and II. New York: American Historical Society, Inc., 1930.

Leader, June 28, 1956.

Literary Digest, April 7, 1900.

Little, Jack. Articles. *South Monmouth News* and *Ocean County Leader*, 1951.

Manasquan 1887–1987. Compiled by the Centennial History Book Committee. Edited by Wesley V. Banse. Topeka, KS: Jostens Publishing Co., 1988.

Manasquan, New Jersey. Compiled by Townfolk for the Diamond Jubilee. Sponsored by the Manasquan Chamber of Commerce, 1962.

McCormick, Richard P. *New Jersey from Colony to State*. Princeton, NJ: D. Van Nostrand Co. Inc., 1964.

Minutes of the Brielle Borough Council. 1919.

Neary, John "Pete." "The Civil War Era." In *The History of Brielle: Union Landing Revisited*. Brielle, NJ: Union Landing Historical Society Inc., 1989.

New Jersey Tercentenary Almanac.

"On the Green." Club publication, n.d.

Outlook, September 7, 1901.

Pearce, Winifred. "Fond Memories of Brielle." Paper submitted to the Brielle Library, 1960.

Phillips, Ralph D. "The Lenape Indians." In *The History of Brielle: Union Landing Revisited*. Brielle, NJ: Union Landing Historical Society Inc., 1989.

Pierce, Arthur D. *Smuggler's Woods*. New Brunswick, NJ: Rutgers University Press, 1960.

Point Pleasant Ledger, June 28, 1956.

Pstrak, Gary. "History of Brielle Fire Company #1."

Rose, T.F., and T.T. Price. *Historical and Biographical Atlas of the New Jersey Coast*. Philadelphia: Woolman & Rose, 1878.

Salter, Edwin. *A History of Monmouth and Ocean Counties*. Bayonne, NJ: E. Gardner and Son, 1890.

Sloane, Eric. *Our Vanishing Landscape*. New York: Wilfred Funk, Inc., 1955.

Smith, Barbara Carver, CGRS, RG. *The Longstreet Family of Monmouth County, New Jersey*. Compiled for the Monmouth County Park System, 1983.

Turner, Harry J. "Brielle, Its Beginnings." Paper submitted to the Brielle Library, 1960.

Unknown newspaper, 1924.

Wall Township 1671–1964. Wall Township Tercentenary Committee, 1964.

Weiss, Harry B., and Grace M. Weiss. *The Revolutionary Salt Works of the New Jersey Coast*. Trenton, NJ: Past Times Press, 1959.

Winters, Helen Leavens. "A Flapper at the Jersey Shore." Unpublished manuscript.

Wood, Don, Joel Rosenbaum and Tom Gallo. *The Unique New York and Long Branch Railroad*. Earlton, NY: Audio-Visual Designs, 1985.

Visit us at
www.historypress.net